Don't Get Excited But...

Rev. David Hazeldine

© 2023 David Hazeldine

49 Kingmere, South Terrace
Littlehampton, BN17 5LD, United Kingdom
www.freedompublishing.net

ISBN: 978-1-908154-66-8

British Library Cataloguing in Publication Data. A catalogue record for this
book is available from the British Library

Unless otherwise stated all scripture quotations are taken from the New
International Version

Formatted by Freedom Publishing
Cover artwork by Ellie O'Connor
Cover layout by Sharon O'Connor
Printed in the United Kingdom

Table of Contents

Introduction

This is a true story. I wish the tragedy that befell me and in turn our family wasn't true and that it didn't really happen - but it did. However, I'm glad the outcomes of strengthened love, faith, and purpose are true and remain so to this day. There are also numerous good outcomes mentioned in this story for mine and Sam's families in that we have all in some way ended up better off than when we started. Therefore, after reading our story, if you were to ask me "David, are you saying you are glad this tragedy happened to you?" I'd be faced with a quandary: can I say "Yes," and have the outcomes without the strokes? I'm not sure I can.

I now live on a plain of thankfulness that few know. I wish many could taste it too but I don't want them to experience it because they would have to go through something similar to what I went through in order to experience it, and I wouldn't wish that on anyone. The sweetest things in life often come after the taste of suffering and so it proved to be in my case.

I think my story is worth telling primarily because it brings hope out of devastation, not the 'cross your fingers' definition of hope we use colloquially but the biblical hope of certainty based on faith. It took me two years' worth of afternoons to write this book one handed (for reasons that will become clear in the book) because I believe so much in the power of this hope. I could have authored this book in several different ways, drawing out different themes, and they would all be true. But I chose to write it this way because the impact of The Voice's words and Sam's devotion on my recovery came through the strongest to me. It could have been about determination, positivity, and exercise. It could have been written as a manual for therapists on their care from a patient's perspective and there are touches of these, but love, faith, and purpose chimed loudest for me.

I never felt our love for each other ever lacked anything. Sam and I have always been happily married and yet throughout the pages of this book you'll see our discovery of a deeper love we never knew possible. The biggest question I had about marital love (and I know others have it too) I had unknowingly given up hope of ever receiving an answer to. Through this tragedy I'm fortunate to have received the answer to it and now know something of a love I never conceived was possible.

Whether my faith was intact was the first thing I remember Sam asking me about after my tragedy. Though I couldn't express it at the time I felt alarm about this. Many turn away from belief in a deity when bad things happen but I felt prepared for such suffering and turning away from my lifelong faith in Jesus truly never once entered my mind. I had been studying deeply the pages of scripture regarding suffering in the decade leading up to my tragedy and had wrestled with and come through the arguments that can cause people to stumble. The book though does outline my particular struggles with the physical and mental pain of suffering and how I dealt with them.

This book is written for Christians and people of all faiths and none. It is also written for those who are agnostic and those who are spiritually aware (on reflection, that basically means everyone), though it is obviously written from my Christian minister's viewpoint. The book includes my personal thoughts, views, feelings, perspectives, and reactions at the time, whether good or bad, because there is always a story to be told in the journey through them. I should also say that the therapists' involvement in my story and their written perspectives on my recovery in no way serve as their endorsement of the Christian faith. I've preserved their privacy as I said I would and have done this by naming them according to their unique features that I fondly remember them by. Close friends and family have been named because I know they don't mind being named.

The final main theme that pervades all the pores of this book is purpose. Purpose can see you through the darkest of times if you know why things are happening. It enables you to make sense of life, find joy in your labours, receive vision for a better future, and removes the crippling power of comparison and jealousy from your life. It is so powerful a wise man once said that if you don't have it you will perish. I've thankfully had a general sense of purpose all my life leading me on but I've never quite known *exactly* what that purpose was for. I am happy to report this tragedy conclusively clarified this for me.

I pray through reading this book you'll discover a renewed understanding of love, faith, and purpose in whatever circumstance you find yourself. May the God I believe in have mercy on you.

Thanks

When lying in my hospital bed in Lewisham, locked-in and totally paralysed, I had a lot of time to think. One of those thoughts was 'I've got a lot of people to thank.' That list of people to thank has got longer since that initial thought.

People I know who have prayed and are still praying for my family and I, people I don't know who have prayed, people who have practically helped, and people who have done both. People of no faith who have heartily wished us well, and even old school friends who have held us in their thoughts – to you all our family is eternally grateful.

Special thanks goes to Sam, Sophie, and Samuel, whose love, devotion, encouragement, help, patience, and understanding have been unspeakably outstanding throughout. Immeasurable thankfulness is felt by us all to our corresponding families who prayed, cared, and financially helped us resettle near to them in our beloved Surrey.

To my wonderful church family in Belvedere, who I was so swiftly removed from, we are indebted to your love and will miss you dearly in our new lives – Ephesians 1:15-16.

Warmest thanks go to our friend Bettina Potts, whose gift of a diary to Sam so she could write things down and remember what clinicians were telling her inadvertently made this book possible.

Thanks to Sam's boss Martina Hunt, whose compassion, understanding, and foresight made it possible for Sam to devote herself to me.

When we were suddenly thrown into the biggest crisis of our lives and instinctively rallied round each other to survive, we inadvertently though understandably, were unable to stay in contact with several of our closest friends for a time. Without fail they all have stayed faithful at a distance to us and I'm pleased to say now the worst of the crisis is over and the pandemic is also loosening its grip on the UK we've now reconnected with them. For that we're truly thankful.

To all the health care assistants, doctors, nurses, therapists, and consultants at St Georges Hospital, Tooting, at The Princess Royal Hospital, Orpington, at University Hospital, Lewisham, at The Royal Hospital for Neuro-disability, Putney, at St Peter's Hospital, Chertsey, at Queen Mary's Hospital, Roehampton, and to my local community therapists – thank you for helping put me back together so professionally, amid a pandemic – your job has been my life. I trust this book goes some small way to acknowledging the role you all played in supporting my family and I throughout our ordeal.

Special appreciation goes to my niece Ellie O'Connor, for her front cover artwork and to her mother Sharon (Big Sis) O'Connor, who is Sam's sister and my sister-in-law, for her cover design. Special thanks also to my brother Stuart, who helped me with his scriptwriting experience in the final drafts of this book – I hope I did his notes justice. Sophie, Clare Constant, and Freedom Publishing helped greatly with their dispassionate editing too. Thanks also to Jim Penberthy for the encouragement to write and the introduction to Freedom Publishing.

And now to my Lord and Saviour Jesus Christ, 'The Voice,' may I spend the rest of my days telling everyone of Your great mercy.

One

Something's Supposed to Happen

Within the space of twelve hours without any prior warning, this forty-six-year-old Baptist Church minister suffered four simultaneous strokes and became so severely disabled that neurological consultants told my wife I had 10%-20% chance of survival. Survival meant living on a ventilator for life in an institution. Our family, our faith, and our purpose seemed devastated beyond all recognition. How had things so suddenly and unexpectedly come to this?

Way Back When

"...in sickness and in health..." she vowed to me. Four-hundred people heard her promise it on the 13th of March 1993 in the picturesque church of my childhood village in Surrey, South-East England. Why was she willing to make such vows to me? I'm just an average guy: yes, I was driven in life, but so were others; I was athletic just like many lads I knew; I was devoted to my faith too, but I was surrounded by people like that. Yet for some reason that I could never quite work out nineteen-year-old Samantha Jane O'Connor loved me, twenty-year-old David Garry Hazeldine and that made me the happiest guy in the world.

We'd both grown up in the same village, me with my loving, church-going family of Mum and Dad, Stuart and Mark, and Sam in an equally loving family of non-church-going Mum, Dad, and sister Sharon. We didn't go to the same schools growing up either so seemed destined not to meet. But when she and her parents started investigating spirituality and attending our small church we first saw each other.

The church met in a community centre and didn't have its own baptism pool. So when a few of us wanted to get baptised we had to use another local Baptist church's pool, and Sam and her parents came along to the baptismal service to see what it was all about. I remember seeing Sam, with her English Rose features, looking on. 'She looks too old to be friends with me' I thought, being only fourteen then. Afterwards, we went back to someone's house for a celebration and awkwardly bumped into each other on the top of a child's climbing frame. We only had that awkward teenage 'first time' acknowledgement which I put down to her being older.

A few months passed and Stuart and I left that small community church to attend a much bigger Baptist church in the nearby town that had a large youth group, leaving my much younger brother Mark, my parents, and Sam and her family behind. A while later though her parents felt Sam should also mix with other Christian young people and turned up at our new church to check out the youth group. I'd obviously had my growth spurt in that time because when she came smiling through the front door I thought 'Oh, she's the same age as me, I'd better introduce her to the youth group.' From that day on we became firm friends.

When I turned sixteen I was thinking of asking a particular girl out. Seemingly from nowhere it also popped into my mind that I should ask Sam out instead. I recoiled at the idea. There was no way I was going to ruin our friendship over 'teen relationship issues,' because I couldn't imagine my life without Sam in it. Wait! Did I just say I couldn't imagine my life without Sam in it? The gravity of what I'd just thought hit me and I made a momentous decision there and then: I'm going to marry Sam.

She Knew What She Was Getting

Since I can remember I've been involved in church. I was in dramatic productions from a young age led by my mum, then street theatre as a teenager which I loved just as much. Stuart and I sang in a church children's choir, and Mark and I often played music together at home for fun. Mark played drums whilst I played the guitar and when we grew older we both played in church settings independently. My dad, a very logical and stimulating man, taught me in Sunday school. He always illustrated Bible stories with maps and pictures to bring them alive.

With those influences on me I learned to love creative forms of expression, particularly preaching because it drew on all my dramatic experiences of storytelling, body language, and expression – little did I know then that someday I'd only be able to communicate with my eyelids. On the other hand, Sam was a shrinking violet who hated the limelight, apart from when she danced. She'd loved ballet since she was two and sometimes went to classes three times a week. But that stopped when I came along – not my fault honest.

Not only did Mum express her spirituality creatively but she was also very practical with it. She was forever helping people in need and showing mercy often at great cost to her own time. We helped Irish travellers who had no water, raised money door-to-door for Christian Aid, and I spent hours waiting in the car as she visited isolated old people. Helping people just rubbed off on me without realising it.

This was all in the intolerant social climate of the 1980s where if you held a view which people didn't like they let you know about it. Countless times I was picked on for my faith: spat on by younger kids, thrown over fences by 'mates,' shouted at by neighbours for helping "those gypsy people," mocked by teachers, and Stuart and I were both constantly insulted as 'God squad' or 'Bible bashers.' It just made me more determined to examine my spiritual side more deeply and see if it was worth holding against these pressures – it was.

I was so convicted about its message that at aged sixteen I took on the leadership of our school's tiny Christian Union. I began by running a couple of lunch time meetings in the main hall and invited the whole school by promoting them in assemblies and putting posters up everywhere. I preached for the first time at those two meetings for anyone interested in Christianity and to my surprise, that little Christian Union grew to about a hundred people in one week. It settled back down to about sixty people by the end of the year, but even so, from five to sixty was pretty amazing to me. Something had happened that was beyond my ability. It wasn't only me who recognised this but others too, and I got invited to speak at a few larger gatherings in the area to encourage others in their faith-filled endeavours by sharing my experience. My expectations were set for life after that experience - I found my calling. I wanted to spend my life and give my heart and soul to spreading the Christian message.

Sam also knew she was getting a competitive husband who loved sports. A typical day for me was to cycle a paper round before school, come home and do weight training before cycling to school. When there I'd play football before, during, and after school. Then cycle home for some more weight training and off out round the beautiful Surrey countryside for fun. Then I'd come home for tea, play snooker against Dad, go to sleep and do it all again the next day. My attitude was typified by one memorable event at school sports day when I was fourteen.

It was getting towards the end of the day and the track events were over. The crowd had migrated to the few remaining field events. I'd already won the triple jump and only the long jump was left, but there was more at stake than just winning the event itself. If anyone got over five metres they'd qualify for the Surrey trials. The only thing was my best jump ever at that point was only four metres seventy-five. And that's not all, my good friend at the time was also in the competition and he was faster and springier than me. He'd leapt over four metres seventy-five a few times. So not only was there a crowd watching, but if anyone were going to qualify it would be him.

He was about to take his last attempt but had not yet leapt the qualifying distance of five metres. He rocketed down the runway, leapt high in the air to the crowd's cheer and landed in the sand pit. The teacher announced loudly to rapturous applause "Five metres thirty." My heart sunk. He was through to the trials. I now had the last jump of the competition, and all eyes were on me. Instead of crumbling under the pressure though, I found myself turning all that nervous energy into excitement. It was my first taste of the spirit of challenge; 'What if I can do this?' I thought.

I pelted down the runway like there was no tomorrow, hit the board smack on and hung in the air like a crunched-up ball for what seemed like ages. I did the longest leg shoot ever, almost landing on my bottom. "Five metres ten" I looked at my PE teacher's smiling face and he said those words I'll never forget "You're through!"

That wasn't all Sam was getting though. She was getting a man devoted to listening prayer. It was a strange thing that someone so outgoing, so gregarious, and competitive as me should be drawn to times of great contemplation and silence. But after an unexpected powerful experience one night in my bedroom, later witnessed by Mum and Stuart, the church 'God' of my family who always seemed so distant came near. I experienced a new intimacy in my faith that has been with me from that day to this.

Throughout my teenage life I found myself being inwardly drawn to quiet places, my favourite of which was a particular tree just a stone's throw from my house. I was hidden there (no passers-by ever looked up), undistracted from life and free to pray. I didn't talk much but rather just listened to God for hours at a time.

It seemed entirely rational to me that if I'd been given ears, He'd want me to listen to His voice. When I believed I'd heard The Voice, I'd know a deep calmness inside and a divine closeness that was difficult to explain with human language. It would be like time standing still. On occasion it was so inwardly indelible that it had the power to drown out all other voices no matter who's they were or what they were saying. I believed it was The Voice who told me to run those lunch time meetings at school, much to my peers' surprise, and I think that's probably why they went so well.

On Christmas Eve of 1989 I asked Sam out instead of that other girl. She never said 'Yes' though, she just inter-locked her arm with mine and rested her head on my shoulder. 'I was waiting for you to say that' she said with her trademark smiley face. She later told me she'd been waiting for me for well over a year.

In the coming days we both openly started talking about love and what that meant. From what little understanding we had of it then, we agreed that love meant 'forever.' And so we wouldn't say 'I love you' unless we were ready for marriage.

A few months later on March 13th we first said 'I love you' to each other, and that's why Sam chose that date in 1993 for our marriage. I know we were young getting married, but my calling to church work was so strong that I didn't want to wait for a few years then get married and for that girl to not know how my calling had been formed. Since that powerful experience in my bedroom, confirmed in my first preaching efforts, I'd had a deep sense in my heart that something significant was going to happen in my ministry and I wanted Sam involved in it from the start.

Journeys

With my best friend on my arm and a passion to communicate the Christian message, we left Surrey with high expectations and joined a church in West Sussex where I could do just that. It's where we met Clive and his wife Jane, who became friends we've known ever since. Bizarrely, the garden Sam and I first awkwardly met in turned out to be his uncle's - small world. They led the youth work back then and Sam and I volunteered alongside them for six great years.

My expectations were met and heightened when we started to run youth meetings all over the country encouraging young people to really take their faith seriously and make a positive difference in their communities. Something was happening again that was beyond me, and I was loving it. But in prayer one day The Voice said that I needed to do youth work full-time and eventually we ended up in Loudwater, High Wycombe where I became a Church of England youth pastor.

My ministry developed there from purely youth work to leading the youth and some of the church into a community visitation project. It was not what I had expected but was very fulfilling and exciting, nonetheless. I had wanted to see the youth group grow in numbers like my school Christian union had but saw my ministry going in a new direction. Initially I was confused, but on reflection was consoled by how the young people themselves had grown in their faith and impacted the community through our project.

Circumstances conspired favourably and I landed a career in community work at the local council and in our spare time Sam and I set about fresh community projects in a council estate in town, looking again for community transformation. We gave our all to that for five years at great financial and physical cost and helped a lot of people in dire circumstances. I remember one time scraping up piles of dog poo from around a lady's garden who had severe mental health problems, 'If this is what it takes' I thought. I wondered if a church might even form out of the work because a small community of spiritual people was gathering around our projects, but after three years of trying it never really got off the ground in a sustainable way. It seemed like humans were doing all the work and we lacked that 'something' outside ourselves like I'd had at school and travelling round the country with Clive. I was beyond frustrated this time, crestfallen even. Though many lives were helped, not being able to build a church round the community projects meant we couldn't help grow them spiritually and this hit me hard. We'd even had the great support of nearby Goldhill Baptist for some years and I still couldn't get things off the ground.

I fasted forty days to prayerfully listen for clarity on this. Why had my youth ministry unexpectedly changed direction into community work? Why had my expectations not been met in establishing a church in this old council estate? I gained no real clarity throughout except that if I was to do that kind of thing again I should be ordained.

Ordained? It did not sit comfortably with me then and certainly wasn't on my agenda. Sam and I were religious in terms of our weekly church attendance, but we weren't exactly your religious type, as I perceived ordained vicars to be back then. For example, our little group of people in the old council estate that gathered around our community projects met in a bar and I preached in jeans and a T-shirt. Over the years we'd become used to exploring spirituality with the kind of people who'd never darken the doors of an established church, those who have no airs or graces and say it how it is.

Getting ordained would mean sacrifice again, but not just for me and Sam but also for our children Sophie, 9, and Samuel, 4. We might have to move away affecting their schooling and friendships. Financially, we'd be hit hard as I was dropping down to a part-time church salary and Sam would have to get a part time job. I spoke with Sam later that same day about ordination and she just smiled at me and said, "Yup, I think that's right." She seemed willing to follow me again on yet another journey. And maybe my expectations of what could be achieved in communities through the Christian message would be met through the ministry of an established church. Maybe that was what was missing before? And I'd be full-time at it and not a volunteer, so that might help.

Unsurprisingly, I was rejected from ordination the first time by a committee in Goldhill Baptist Church, apparently I 'wasn't the kind of person typical established churches would want to lead them.' But I wasn't perturbed, I knew I'd heard correctly in prayer. I told the minister of the church this had happened, and he was outraged. "The church of the future needs activists like you in leadership!" he exclaimed. He saw to it that the decision was overturned and shortly after a small Baptist church in Totteridge, High Wycombe took me on. The kids weren't affected by any move, and I started on the journey of ordination training in September 2009. My expectations were rising again because things were falling into place.

Frustration

I loved my training at Oxford University and loved my work in Totteridge. They were lovely, dedicated people and I enjoyed their support. I needed to draw on all my skills of communication in preaching and playing music and use my experience of youth work too. A nice community of faith-seekers was being built up around the fringes of church life, and we updated a lot of the facilities, but I felt held back by necessary church administration and meetings and the results I was getting in ministry didn't meet my expectations considering the effort I was putting in. Like my youth work and community projects before, my expectations weren't being met. My efforts weren't enough for what was needed, and I couldn't really grow the church numerically, let alone see any kind of community transformation. I was burning out.

I'd have thought this was a mid-life crisis, but this was a repetitive cycle since early adult life in High Wycombe. By this time I'd just reached my forties and cut a frustrated figure. The middle-aged spread was settling in, and I was getting a bit thinner on top. I was losing some of my youthful fire and my motivation was slipping a bit because things weren't working out as expected even though I was doing what I thought I was being led to do. But there was one salve to the situation that helped a bit.

Property Development

To make the full-time position as minister of Totteridge viable, we had to move into the church house. We could no longer afford to pay our mortgage which was not a nice feeling, but we took it as an opportunity and tried our hand as landlords for the first time.

Sam and I had stumbled into property development years earlier and used it as an extra source of income, because when Sophie and Samuel came along our low paid jobs didn't cover everything our burgeoning family needed. Sam would find a wreck of a house for a bargain price which had potential, then over a few years myself and builders would renovate it. I loved the physical and creative challenges of it all. I'd rip out the old and the builders would construct the new, installing all of Sam's shrewd fittings and fixture bargains. Both Sophie and Samuel got used to living amongst building dust and ripped out kitchens. Over the years they never complained, in fact they almost expected it.

When it came to the houses Sam had an eye for a bargain. When she was a child going round the supermarket shelves, her late mum said that any money she saved through coupons she could keep. Being brought up like that and learning to haggle over pennies at car boot sales gave her a keen eye for a bargain. I also loved realising potential – just like in people, communities, and churches I guess.

We reached the stage where we just couldn't buy a house that didn't need renovating. We only wanted to live in a house with our own stamp on it. Our speciality became bungalows. They had such potential to realise in their large plots and cavernous lofts and because they were usually outdated they could often be bought at a bargain price.

Mercy

We'd been in High Wycombe now for seventeen years and we'd given our heart and soul for that place. But I'd got so low after six years of ordained ministry that one morning I couldn't face getting out of bed. I'd worked so hard for unfulfilled expectations and was physically, mentally, and spiritually exhausted. For the first time ever in my life I was questioning my faith.

The questioning went on for months. It involved many tears (I'm not ashamed to say) and at times it seemed I was facing an abyss. My faith that I'd built my life upon was shaken because I'd put my heart and soul into everything I'd done up till now, put our family's life on the line and sacrificed a lot, but my expectations were not being met time and again.

Much study and pondering followed. Where was the God of my youth when my expectations were met and even superseded? Ever since then I'd lived with the notion that something beyond myself was supposed to happen at every juncture to make my endeavours succeed but I just seemed to struggle through with the odd blip of success. Frustration and confusion was all-consuming after the effort and sacrifice I'd put in and I was getting irritable around the home and sometimes frustrations boiled over for innocuous reasons.

Early one morning, I got to the point when I realised I couldn't carry on in ministry like this. I prayed, "I'm working so hard for You, just give me a break or I'm going to break. Have mercy on me." It wasn't a threat, just a reality. There were no angels, no Hollywood choirs in response, just a moment of divine clarity where I realised it was also me that needed to be helped and transformed, not just communities. It had taken over twenty years for me to run out of steam, but now I was ready to receive mercy and be helped.

I started to come out of that depressing time gradually and falteringly because it took years to change habits of a lifetime. But I also came out of it with a new understanding that began a revolution in me – the Christian God was a merciful God. I no longer needed to strive to make something happen, He was going to help me, and it would be much easier that way. I didn't need to give my life as some kind of sacrifice for me to win and to make things in church life work, but I could ask for His help to fulfil my calling, even in the face of my failings, mistakes, misperceptions, and misunderstandings. Mercy is divine help for those who don't deserve it, and that was me. I was starting to see my whole life through a different lens now, things were becoming clearer. It was not about competing or winning to be the best but about being helped by The Best and helping others. I had to be brought to the end of myself to realise it though. I was consciously open to receiving His mercy now.

'The Big Smoke'

There were some practical changes I needed to make to reduce the frustrations I was feeling too. We needed a decent income, we needed a change of scenery, and we needed to get back to some energising property development, not renting, to balance out the sometimes-draining work of day-to-day church ministry.

We were facing a window of opportunity with the kids schooling because of their ages, now sixteen and ten, which meant if I didn't make those changes now we'd have to stay in High Wycombe for at least another five years, and I knew I couldn't do that. It would not be good for me or Sam.

Work wise we both felt the time was right for Sam to start building her career now the kids were older. She was so capable but had willingly prioritized the kids schooling and my calling over her career. We always saw ourselves as a team and fell into our roles to facilitate the growth of our family. She was trained as an executive secretary and worked in that field until we came to Wycombe but had been out of full-time work whilst Sophie and Samuel were younger.

She took on a little part-time admin job in town with the local police force with an eye to going full-time if the role developed. Within four weeks she'd received a quadruple promotion. The police commander had heard how organised and professional she was and took her as his own personal assistant full-time. It was fantastic. She was clearly seen as very capable by others and not just me and could do so much more given the right opportunity.

With that in mind I started looking around for new ministry opportunities. I'd initially started sniffing around in our favoured home of Surrey. With its leafy roads, Hampton Court Palace, and the beautiful River Thames, it held many fond teenage memories for us. But nothing came of the feelers I put out and instead we both found ourselves being led towards the 'Big Smoke' of London. It would be a real departure for us all from Buckinghamshire but would provide Sam with the fantastic job opportunities I knew she was capable off.

A ministry position arose in Belvedere, in the South-East London Borough of Bexley, which was closer to Sam's widowed father in Ramsgate and not too far from the rest of both our families still based in Surrey. The local Baptist church there were looking for a new minister and all the right conditions I was looking for were there. Schooling was close by, Sam could get into central London if she needed to (and she did, she got a job in Westminster), the church was numerically much bigger meaning I wouldn't have to do everything, and they were offering a good-sized house as well. The church members were irreligious in their church style and were already reaching out to the community in practical ways. I could tell there was untapped potential in the people and in their dated, unused buildings too. It had my name written all over it.

We left High Wycombe and the people at the church there with heavy hearts but were excited for the change. We fitted right in and then bought a little wreck of a flat to do up which took my mind off the usual day-to-day responsibilities of ministry.

Sam had said upon our arrival in Belvedere that she could tell that we would only be there for a short time, which I thought was very odd. I was prepared to see Samuel, only eleven then, right through to university at least. I filed her thought away as I'd learned early on in our marriage not to dismiss any of Sam's thoughts, being the sharp cookie she is.

Sure enough, during my sabbatical (two years into the role) that feeling of 'something's supposed to happen' re-emerged, with me getting bogged down in necessary admin again and not making the gains I felt were possible in ministry. I felt we just needed some divine help.

I revisited her earlier comments about being here for a short while and asked her why she had said them: "Somethings going to happen for you here, David" she just re-affirmed, not alleviating my confusion. I was trusting more in mercy and not trying too much myself. But I couldn't deny that my frustrations were rising again, and I could sense despondency creeping back in that something beyond me in the church and community didn't seem to be happening on the scale I knew it could – where was the God of my youth?

Part of my confusion was that I had to accept that maybe Sam and I were just plain wrong about what we thought we sensed. After all, life was good. Maybe we were just greedy? Sam's work/life balance was great (she was even able to work from home next to me every Friday), the schools were okay, church was moving forward and impacting the community through projects, and we were realising potential in the people and buildings, and we were also enjoying the charms of London life.

So this time I knew I had to be pro-active about the frustrations early on for everybody's sake but was realistic any changes would merely temporarily ease them. I did two new things: Started looking around for other church roles and wrote a book.

I looked for churches that would move us back to our favoured Surrey. Sam would be able to continue her job in London which she loved and felt very appreciated in, Sophie was already near there at Uni and Sam's elderly father could come and live with us as we'd been saying for a while now. It would fit with GCSEs starting for Samuel too. But how would I tell the church? Three years after arriving I would be off. What would I say? It didn't sit right with me. Fortunately, nothing came of it, so I didn't have to say anything to anyone. But the whole experience left me confused.

The book was called, 'The Majestic Meaning of Mercy.' It strung together my journey of discovery about mercy in greater detail, particularly how it was helping me deal with these inner frustrations, but mainly served as teaching about what the Bible portrays God's mercy to be all about: helping us when we don't deserve it. I knew a lot of ministers and church members had similar desires for community transformation that weren't being fully realised and maybe they could benefit from my experiences.

It took about a year to complete and edit it and was a cathartic experience considering my present frustrations. Throughout writing the book it seemed to me to be the start of a new work; it felt like everything in my life had been building to this point and was now coming together – maybe this was it? Had I found my life's true calling to be communicating the message of mercy, making all that had gone before a precursor? I was now ready to publish it.

Something Happened!

Then, literally two weeks later, something *did* happen – and it wasn't publishing a book. Suddenly and without warning it shook our family to the core leaving us all devastated and we'd all need something beyond ourselves to survive it. Those marriage vows of '…in sickness and in health…' which had hitherto been uncalled upon in our twenty-six-year marriage, would be thrust to the fore. I had been right all along since my youth, something was going to happen in my ministry, but neither Sam nor I quite expected *this*.

Sam, 19, David, 20, getting married on 13th March, 1993

Two

Something Happened

Waking up very early was not unusual for me, but Saturday the 2nd of November 2019 was a bit different. Ever since my teenage paper round days I'd remained an early riser. With no distractions in those wee small hours I found it easier to listen in prayer. If it were incredibly early I'd go back to bed afterwards but if like that day it was around 6am I'd stay up for the day after I'd finished. Only that day was a bit different because I woke with an unexplained headache. Just a dull one but a weird one. It was aching all over my head particularly at the back near the neck. I took some Ibuprofen and thought it would be too distracting for prayer, so I went back to bed to let it pass.

Waking a few hours later the headache was still there, not particularly worse though. I thought I should get some paracetamol this time and a drink, maybe it was dehydration. So, with dawn breaking, I pulled back the crumpled duvet and made my way to the bathroom before going downstairs for a drink. As I entered the bathroom, something happened. The hearing in my right ear suddenly went fuzzy and my sight seemed to change weirdly. I lost a bit of balance at the same time and had to steady myself on the door frame. Instantly I knew I needed to lay down because I was a little light-headed. It felt a bit like previous severe flu bouts I'd had where I'd nearly fainted.

I stumbled back to the bedroom across the landing. It was a large landing with five bedrooms and a bathroom off it, so it had a lot of door frames for me to grab on to. As I was heading to the bed, I realised I was building up a bit too much speed. Diving over

Sam on to the bed I just managed to clear her. She was disturbed by it all, but I was just relieved that I hadn't fallen over.

An Inconvenience

Sam needed to get up anyway. She was helping with a craft fair at church. Sam was into crafting, so it was right up her street. Typically churches holding craft fairs were the kind of thing that put me off ordination, usually raising money for a crumbling building or something. I've always felt they should be places of activism where people are helped, where poverty is fought, loneliness eradicated, and the needy helped. They can be places of inspiration and vision.

But this craft fair was different. A ninety-four-year-old lady, who regularly whizzed past my house on her mobility scooter, wanted to bring the community together. Brexit had happened, Trump was in the White House and society in our two nations was becoming divided. And she wanted to do something about it which I thought was rather cool. She had booked the church hall soon after I arrived at Belvedere and, two years later, today was the day – just as well she was still alive. We'd already done some set up the night before and this morning Sam and I said we'd help with some heavy things that needed to be lifted.

We still had time to watch a recording of some late-night TV from the night before in the hope that when it had finished my headache and other symptoms would have eased. But they hadn't. I tried to stand up to see if I could still help somehow, but I couldn't get my balance. Samuel, as kind as ever, offered to help in my place. Now fifteen he was just starting to sprout and was getting some strength about him which often came in handy. Normally, Sophie used to help but now she was in west London at Uni. So off they drove together to the church leaving me resting.

In bed I tried to rationalise things, 'If I get to twelve o'clock and I'm still not well enough I'll have to ring Mick and get him to run the service tomorrow. He'll need some emergency preparation time.' 'What can this be: A migraine? An infection of some sort?' I wondered. I needed to go to the loo so staggered there and back. Whatever it was it wasn't going away.

Time passed and it reached twelve o'clock, so I rang Mick from my bed and asked him to cover for me. After the usual banter he agreed. A tall man of retirement age, well respected in the church and the community, he'd taken voluntary redundancy years earlier and was now busier than ever. He did loads of outreach stuff through the church. I'd gone full-time into property development years earlier to do the same thing as him. We had similar passions and were equally disdainful of religion and what its ugliness could do to a church. He was one of the reasons I joined Belvedere Baptist Church.

Sam and Samuel had come back by now and she got me a few sandwiches. For some reason I started to feel heavier and had to prop myself up on my elbow with pillows for extra support so I could eat them. To prevent things from becoming any more inconvenient for everyone at church today or tomorrow we decided to call 111 and see if we could find out what was going on and get it sorted.

Sam explained my symptoms to them, and they said they'd arrange for the paramedics to come. Samuel was in the room at this time and came over to the bed side. In his low teenage voice he queried, "What's up Dad?" "I don't know, but something's not right." I replied in my now faint, strained voice. Though I could think and rationalise things it seemed my head wasn't as clear as it was normally and I couldn't work out why. I'd never had these symptoms before.

Lewis Hamilton

Waiting for the paramedics took a while. I decided to watch the Formula 1 qualifying session as I normally would the day before the race. Lying down in my bed was the best position because I was steady and I could see the television from there.

The British racer Lewis Hamilton could become World Champion for the sixth time the next day in Austin, Texas, if he finished eighth place or higher in the race. He was the master of his own destiny making this qualifying session for race day start position not as crucial as a normal one. Just as well because he qualified uncharacteristically in fifth. Being interested in most sports this took my concentration off the symptoms and the programme was over two hours long so we assumed the paramedics would arrive by then. But after the programme had finished there was no sign of them. Feeling a bit perturbed Sam rang 111 again to try and escalate matters and they assured her they would.

The paramedics took four hours to arrive from when Sam first rang, so all hopes of attending the long awaited and much anticipated craft fair were long gone. Samuel went off with his mate and his mum for a planned sleepover which was a weight off our minds.

The paramedics entered the bedroom with their high viz jackets rustling and a jovial tone in their voices. They kindly explained that my symptoms were not life threatening, so I had been pushed down their list. 'Reassuring to know' I thought. They remained calm throughout but were not sure what the symptoms meant. They barraged me with questions which Sam helped to answer because for some reason I was getting a little slower in my reaction times and in my speech. Observations of my vital signs were taken; blood pressure fine, oxygen levels good, pulse all right. Standing around the bedside they calmly discussed options of what to do and settled on the fact that it was probably some kind of infection, but to be sure they said it was best to attend Accident and Emergency and let them find out.

They asked Sam if she could drive me in, but by that time she could barely support me and wasn't sure she could even get me to the car. It was decided they'd take me in the ambulance with Sam following. She was hopeless with directions much to our family's amusement, so she double-checked the Sat Nav co-ordinates with them just in case we got separated. We were going to Woolwich hospital where I'd done many a pastoral visit.

I was too dodgy on my feet to walk down the stairs. I slid down them on my bottom and the male paramedic helped me out the door into the evening darkness and into the back of the waiting ambulance. The engine was running but no flashing lights. I was guided onto the patient trolley, and he sat across from me.

I knew it wouldn't take too long to get there and we exchanged pleasantries on the way there and got to the usual part in the conversation where he (like many others) asked me what I did for a living. "I'm a vicar." I'd had this type of conversation before and it always draws the same response; "Oh, you don't look or talk like one" and sure enough he reacted in the same way. I'd been around builders a bit, loved sport and was well built so didn't fit most people's picture of one.

At that point in our chat to avoid the usual blank expressions, I didn't tell him I was in fact a Baptist Church minister. I couldn't stand being called a vicar because of all the religious stereotypes. But people's confusion over my preferred title had ground me down, so I'd just say "Yeah, a vicar" and shrugged it off like it was the first time I'd ever heard it.

Something Happened

We arrived at Accident and Emergency in about twenty minutes, the entrance of which was shining its light out into the night sky ahead of us. The paramedic helped me get my balance and held me up as we walked towards the door. 'This looks different in the dark' I thought. Bizarrely, I'd been to that entrance to the hospital only once before - the previous day. I'd taken a dyslexic, homeless alcoholic there who was going yellow with jaundice. I'd got to know him quite well over the previous year and managed to get him off the streets with the help of a charity worker.

All this was going through my mind whilst trying to remain standing because I felt so heavy now. We got to the entrance and the paramedic reached for a wheelchair that unbeknownst to me he pulled up right behind me. Sam had fortunately arrived at the same time and had gone to the reception to sign me in - typical Sam, always handling the admin. The Chinese male receptionist spoke loudly across the Saturday evening hum of the busy Accident and Emergency department. "Are you David Hazeldine?" For some reason I couldn't speak, so just nodded. And before I had time to think about my loss of speech I blacked out. In the split second it took for my eyes to shut I collapsed backward and felt myself slumping into what I could tell was a wheelchair. 'That was lucky,' I thought. "Who put that there?" At the same time, what seemed like water ran up over the left side of my throat 'What's that?' I thought. Then unconsciousness.

Three
Intensive Care Experience

The following is exactly what it was like for me coming out of unconsciousness and exactly how it happened in the order things happened. These were my thoughts at the time as I remember them. If there are thoughts and feelings you think I must have had about waking up to find I'm totally paralysed and suffering locked-in syndrome (consciously aware but trapped in your own body only able to blink) and wonder why I've not recorded them, it's because I simply didn't have those thoughts. All I knew was what I was hearing and feeling – or not feeling as the case was.

The gaps in the text represent unknown periods of time that I recollect. There were others I'm told but the staff were playing with my levels of sedation to administer the most accurate levels of care which made me unaware of time. Remember, the last thing I'd been told by human beings was that I probably had an infection.

I'm awake. That darkness is the inside of my eyelids.
"You're going to be okay." That's The Voice (deep calm). Eyelids open. My right eyelid feels heavy. Everything looks a bit funny. This looks like a hospital bay. Those blue curtains are shut around me. What's through that window? (To my right in my peripheral vision.) That sounds like people and the hum of activity. They're whispering. I can't feel anything anywhere – weird, like floating inside and out. I can't talk.

There's two young ladies (coming through the curtains).
"Hello, David."

They are Australian (young, and slim).

"We've been sent in to try and establish communication with you. You're in St George's hospital, London, Neuro-Intensive Care Unit. You've had a brain stem stroke."

I don't know what that means.

"We're going to start very simply. Blinking your eyes once means 'Yes,' blinking twice means 'No.' Do you understand that."

Blink.

"That's good, David. Now can you communicate "No"?"

Blink, Blink. That was simple. "Good, David."

"David, this is an alphabet board. It's got all the letters of the alphabet on it, split between five rows. We want you to spell the word 'Yes' using your eyelids. One blink for 'Yes,' two blinks for 'No.' I'm going to point to the row that has the letter 'Y' in it, and you blink once when I get to the correct row. (She slowly slides her finger down the side of the board whilst watching my eyelids)

Blink.

"Now I'm going to point at each letter slowly until I reach 'Y,' and you blink when I reach it. (She points at each letter and reaches 'Y.')

Blink.

"Very good. Now I'm going to ask you to help me find the next letter, 'E,' starting by finding the correct row. I'm going to run my finger down the left-hand side of the board slowly and when I get to the correct row, you blink once for 'Yes.'

It's going to be the first row, quick blink now. Blink.

"That's good, David. Now let's find the letter 'E' on that row. I'm going to run my finger slowly along the row from left to right and when I arrive at the letter 'E,' blink once for 'Yes.'

"Ready." (she runs her finger along the row)... I blink at 'E.'

"That's correct, David. Now we're going to find the last letter 'S.' Find the row first."

"Ready." (she runs her finger down the left-hand side of the rows... I blink at the correct row.

Now the letter.

"Ready." (she runs her finger along the row till the letter 'S'... I blink.)

"Good, well done, David"

That makes sense.

"Do you have anything you'd like to ask?" Blink.

"OK, David. Let's use that same technique."

How am I going to ask my question, it's so long and has long words? They probably don't know who Lewis Hamilton is or what F1 is. We'll be here ages. I'll have to improvise.

(she starts pointing slowly down the left-hand side for the row.)

Ready... Blink.

"Is this the right row?"

Blink.

(she starts pointing slowly along the row)

Ready... Blink. "Do you mean 'L'?"

Blink.

"Ok, next letter."

Get the row... Blink. "Do you mean the first row?"

Blink.

It's going to be the last letter on the row, wait... Blink.

"Do you mean 'E?'

Blink. We've got this now.

'W,' 'I,' 'S' (using the same method). Wait... "Is that the end of the word?"

Blink.

"Do you mean, Lewis."

Blink.

"Ok, next word"

C-A-R.

"Do you mean car?"

Blink

What are they saying to each other?

"We'll be back shortly."

Oh, they're back.

"Can you hear me, David?"

Blink

"We aren't quite sure what you mean. Do you want to say some more?"

I knew it wouldn't work. Let's do it this way: W-O-R-L-D

"Do you mean 'World'?"

Blink. C-H-A-M-P-I-O-N

"Do you mean 'Champion?'"

Blink.

"We'll be back shortly."

Here they come.

"Yes David, Lewis Hamilton is World Champion."

They're smiling. That's a relief they understood.

This is happening, got no choice. Can't move. Can't feel anything. Processing.

"Leave Belvedere." That's The Voice again. Ah, I am relieved of all that admin. I see now: This is what was meant to happen. No more official meetings. Relief. I'll be able to do more writing and speaking about mercy. Ahh, that's a life's worth of frustration draining away.

There's Sam. Can't turn my head. She's reaching for my right hand and holding it. "Do you still have your faith in the Lord." Of course - Blink.

She wants to read some Bible verses out loud to me.

"New Testament?"

Blink, Blink.

"Old Testament?"

Blink. It's the one where King David says it's better to be at God's mercy in His hands than in mans. She's going through all the books of the Old Testament. Where is it? I just used it in my book. Can't concentrate. Speaking too fast. Need time to think.

"2 Kings?"

Blink. Oh no, that was wrong. What's in 2 Kings? ... King Hezekiah. Where's he? Near the end? I'll have to guess.

"...18, 19, 20."

Blink. If she reads out chapter 20, I'll know.

"In those days Hezekiah became ill and was at the point of death.... 'Remember, LORD, how I have walked before you faithfully and with wholehearted devotion and have done what is good in your eyes.' And Hezekiah wept bitterly.... 'This is what the LORD, the God of your father David, says: I have heard your prayer and seen your tears; I will heal you.'"

That's the wrong one, but it'll do. She'll get the idea.

"How did you know that?!" She's not asking me, she's exclaiming it. She's realising I'm all there.

I didn't mean it, it's the wrong one but it'll do.

Dream: Sam and I are driving at dusk in the West Country. There's an angry sky, but bright sunlight is on the horizon. We're getting near a dual carriageway because I can see rows of streetlamps up ahead. Now we're going into a small cottage. All the people I did ordination training with at Oxford are lying on top of each other making the walls of the house, like cigarettes in their box. How weird. This is a dream. "Nice to see you all and thanks for the meal."

I've got a temperature (I heard a nurse say so). I can't feel it. I can't feel anything. Why don't they sort it out? (they were).

Dream: I'm in Spain, looking at a hotel pool with a fake stone cave and a waterfall over its exit. People are exiting the cave into the main part of the pool in yellow dinghies. They're getting soaked in the waterfall. This must be a dream. Hey, there's my sister-in-law's husband, Dom, and my nephew. They're going under the waterfall and having great fun. Big smiles. Don't the doctors know that if they put me under that waterfall my temperature will go down?

Is this really happening? Can I get up? I'll move my right ankle – it doesn't work. This is happening. Got no choice. It's not a dream. It's really happening.

I'm being wheeled to a halt (in my bed) by the side next to a wall. I wonder what we're waiting for. That's the humdrum of people like in a shopping mall. Am I stationed near a coffee shop in a plaza? Is this a hospital? Do they all know I'm just here behind the plants?

This is happening (Processing).

Dream: This is a big pool of water with stones around the edge, in the middle of a southeast Asian forest. There are people in it. They just dived over the edge down a waterfall into another pool. Now they are walking back up. Don't the doctors know that if they let me dive over the edge my temperature will go down? Oh, this is a dream. Must be drugs or something. Things aren't quite right.

Oh no. It's night-time. These nights are so long. Everything seems wet. There's that bright light they put on in the evenings shining right in my eyes. Things are still busy, but they totally change here at night.

That nurse is leaning in a bit close.

"Am I caring for you well?"

Blink. Does she know what I mean. She's got a plastic visor over her face – strange. Her accent sounds South American, maybe Columbian?

Oh, there's Clive. What's he doing here? It must be bad because he's anointing me with oil. I can't feel his finger though. He's bearing down on me and stretching past wires and pipes to reach me. There's more space on my right side. Clive, I can't talk that's why I'm not saying anything, but I know you're here. He'll agree with The Voice - good.

Now I'm wide awake. They're wheeling me on my bed through Accident and Emergency. People sitting on chairs in rows waiting to be seen. It's night-time and everything's really dark. There are some drink machines lit up. Oh, we're not going down that corridor – I can tell by the spinning ceiling above me. This is a long corridor through some doors – no waiting. Oh, the ceiling's moving quick. I think they just shunted me off my bed onto another surface. I can't feel anything, not even my back on the surface - weird. I'm inside one of those massive scanners, like a big ring all around me. Oh, that's what they sound like, with bits spinning too – like a quiet underground train coming into the station. Interesting. Oh, we're going back now. That was quick. I can see the drinks machine again and from this way I can see everyone's faces now. They're all staring emotionless at me. When you're suffering there's always someone worse than you – oh, I'm that someone who's worse than them.

There's Mark. What else can he do but sit there? No drums and guitar now. I can't talk to you.
    "Do you even know I'm here?"
    He's not sure I'm with it.
    Blink. Do you know I'm communicating with you?

Ah, cold, fresh air on my face. It's daytime and very bright. I'm in the back of an ambulance again. No blue lights so I assume I'm improving. There's someone with me I think, probably another paramedic. Already here? That was quick. They're taking me out of the ambulance – I can tell by the ceiling moving away.

That's what it's like waking up in Neurological Intensive Care and gradually piecing things together through heavy sedation. I had gathered from the nurses, Sam and what I couldn't feel that I was paralysed after a brain stem stroke. Sam told me my body had battled a chest infection which was life threatening due to my vulnerable condition. I was deeply calm throughout though because I'd heard The Voice, so much so I actually asked about Lewis Hamilton's race result instead of reassuring my family. He'd taken the initiative before any human being spoke to me and then later took away all my frustrations that had been bubbling under the surface for so long. I had been there for nine disorientating days.

Four

Unnumbered

The danger of imminent death was passing, and my medical care became more about stabilising me even though the family was still understandably tense. They all had hundreds of rushing thoughts about the implications of what had happened to me whilst still trying to process the severity of it. They knew nothing about brain stem strokes or anything about the other three minor strokes (one each affecting my eyes, ears, and balance) they found out I'd had. Intensive questioning of the consultants, furious googling and YouTube watching, and relentless messaging between each other soon put paid to that.

I didn't have any of that. All I knew was that I couldn't move, talk, eat, feel anything anywhere inside or outside, somehow was going to the loo, yet was deeply calm because I knew I was going to be okay. I found this concoction overwhelming, though not in a bad way but just too much for me to get my head round. It felt like an unexpected breaking wave had just tumbled me over and swirled me around. I had no choice but to go with it knowing eventually it would settle and I could take things in.

How Did They Know?

On Sunday the 10th of November, the ambulance men put me in a private room in Lewisham intensive care ward. I could see through the window in the door that a female nurse stood by a desk on guard 24/7. There was always an update discussion right there between her and visiting family members just before they came in.

There were large, wide windows all along the right side of the room and it was nice to finally see outside into an autumnal London park using my peripheral vision. Life was going on outside and the seasons were still moving, but for me everything stood still. That room was where I first remember seeing Sophie and Samuel. I tracked their movements around my bedside with my eyes, each one taking their turn to talk close to my head. Quite chatty, they seemed calm and happy to see me. My strange environment and physicality consumed me meaning I didn't think for one minute how they would be feeling. Again, Sam told me I'd had a brain stem stroke, but I still didn't really know what that meant. My parents came most days and upon discovering there was a built-in sound system they played some soft contemporary worship music.

They would all tell me about everyone who was praying for me. They had phoned around with the news, taken calls, exchanged texts, and used social media to give updates. There were a number of local Baptist churches around Bexleyheath praying, along with some other denominations, churches in High Wycombe I'd worked in and with, my family's churches, churches in Thanet who my Father-in-law was updating, the 24/7 prayer movement, Clive's church (which had a number of congregations), the Oxford college I went to and all my student friends who were now ordained and leading churches, student missionaries I knew, a Yorkshire church I knew of, churches as far afield as Los Angeles, California and the Philippines who had members I knew, Christian friends all over the world e.g. in Australia, New Zealand, Jerusalem, Croatia, and Nepal. There was also feedback that even a prayer group of little old ladies in Scotland who didn't know me were praying. In their own words my plight even made some of my atheist and agnostic friends pray.

This was overwhelming and wonderful; I was so incredibly thankful and humbled for the unnumbered prayers. But it also made me think about how serious my condition must be because you wouldn't get messages from far-flung places for a cold.

The other thing that made me wonder about the seriousness of my predicament was the fact that people I had hardly spoken to for years were sending lengthy messages of support, one distant school associate even sent a hand-written letter. It sounded like many eulogies from funerals I had presided over – this was bad, almost unbelievably bad. I was just beginning to compute the fact that something so serious had happened to someone like me.

That first night was long. I'd been sleeping and sedated for most of last week, but now I was wide awake. Flat on my back unable to move, I was desperate for some activity to occur. I was bored and I was aching in my right leg with the muscle stiffness that paralysis brings (I didn't realise it then, but this was a good sign that total paralysis was starting to lift). I just needed something to distract me. Then at some point later, one of the two nurses who was giving me round the clock care came over to me. "I'm praying for you; you're going to be okay" she said. Did she know I was a reverend? How did she know I would be okay? It happened twice on successive nights by different nurses. Can they maintain professional integrity and say that? Either way it was encouraging confirmation of what I already knew.

The next night I had a weird, unsettling dream. It had been about successive children needing to play a single musical instrument continuously. The smooth handover between the children involved was crucial because somehow it pertained to my life-or-death. Next morning, after another long, achy night, Sam arrived. "He's off life support" the nurse said. Sam came over and repeated the wonderful news. She probably thought I couldn't hear or understand. I realised then that this was going to be a journey of discovery for Sam. She went on to explain that I had started life support on sixty percent oxygen intake, being able only to breathe forty percent for myself. The handover to decreasing amounts of oxygen had been crucial to my survival. Was that what the dream was about?

Sam was now beaming from ear to ear with this happy news. I saw her wonderful smile again that fills her face and infects you with the joy she's experiencing. The smile reminded me of normality at a time when all around was anything but. She read out an email from my cousin Richard which became a regular feature during my time at Lewisham; they were filled with his glorious sense of humour that seemed to completely ignore my present dilemma. But he knew if I could hear and understand anything at this point I would need some humour, and it took me away elsewhere for a fleeting moment. I was laughing so much inside, but my body was still.

Sam told me yet again that I'd had a brain stem stroke but added that I had also had three others. The doctors were only concentrating on the brain stem one though because it was life threatening. She felt able to say those words 'life threatening' because I was off life support. Was this really happening to me?

I remember feeling like a victim for the first time in my life in that room. My life had been threatened and I wasn't expecting it, worse still, I couldn't do anything about it. I just lay there and took it in. I was galvanising myself. A response of some kind would come as I never took anything lying down (pardon the pun), but for now I was just trying to face up to it. I couldn't yet even spare a thought for my family and the turmoil they were going through because I was mulling things over, just processing the implications.

The following day I was moved to the High Dependency Unit. Somehow I knew this was just to wait for a bay to become available in the specialist stroke ward. All I remember were the grey curtains of the bay into which I was moved and a strange realisation I had. I was looking up all the time. Looking up at ceilings, up at the under-side of door frames, up at people and their chins. Who does that apart from kids? I was lying flat, still, and face up. What a different way from which to see the world. For a guy just a smidgen under six foot this felt strange.

'Seeing' Maple Ward

I was only in that unit for one day before I was moved to Maple Ward, my new home. The bleariness from the sedation was gone, but something was not quite right with my eyesight as I scanned my new surroundings. When I looked left and right, up, and down, things seemed to 'appear,' even though I could see things coming in my peripheral vision. I kind of felt 'not present,' a bit fuzzy in my head. It was like I had a heavy cold or was a bit tipsy. This might be conducive to a good time, but it was all the time. This is how it was going to be for me going forward, discovering my new devastated physicality bit by bit.

As I took in the sights and sounds of my new home I began to slowly look around my room; scanning down my eyes seemed to 'expect' what I'd see – a bit of a shock though when my expectations were wrong. Notable to my standard hospital surroundings was another wall-length row of windows through which I could see the typical London skyline of Victorian architecture. Across from me was a disabled loo which I was too disabled to use and a corridor off our room crammed full down one side with all manner of walking aids, mobile hoists, and one solitary wheelchair. Through my peripheral vision I could see a corridor adjacent to our room through internal glass windows with a desk top computer monitor in it.

Every night was just the same. Long, boring, and painfully achy. I'd manage to stay awake till 8ish but would always wake around 3-4am which is a normal length sleep for me. I'd try and get the nurses' attention to un-ache me when they came by my corpse-like body, but they couldn't hear or see eye blinks. Occasionally they'd notice I was awake, and I'd try and indicate with my eyelids for them to look down at my left foot. It was usually facing inwards and away from me, which looked odd. It would become unbearably achy some nights. I just wanted it turned outwards like the right one. It became a game of 'Guess what David wants' with the night nurses. Touching a part of my body that I could see, they'd wait for one blink or two. Sometimes they'd guess correctly and notice the foot looked odd then move it more outwards, which was sheer bliss. Other times they would just apologetically give up which was demoralising.

I'd learned I had a catheter, which was one of those things I'd never dreamed I'd have. Oddly, it was one of those things that reminded me I was in a bad way – not having locked-in syndrome or being paralysed. The nurse would change my water that hung in a bag up high above me (I was fed through a tube up my nose). Along with changing the catheter bag, that would be some more activity to break up the long nights. They might change the bed position a tiny bit which would relieve the aches for a while. I wasn't laid flat, but my head and torso at 45 degrees and my knees slightly raised like a racing driver, necessary because of feeding. Sometimes two nurses would completely reposition me on sliding sheets – that was the jackpot, pure relief, the best kind of activity.

Dawn couldn't come soon enough, and I would always see out of the wall-length windows the outline of the grey cladded building adjoining ours slowly form out of the darkness. That was pretty much the signal for the night staff to handover to the day staff. The day staff would do their rounds and say 'Hi.' There would be a quick discussion between them about who had been changed, washed, and given new bed clothes. Some moaning if the night staff hadn't changed us, joy if they had.

Being 'changed' would mean first checking if I'd soiled my nappy. It was de-humanising at first, but it soon became expected. Then, rolling me on my side with face pressed against the bed bars, a pair of nurses would whip off the old bed sheets, turn me on to the other side and whip on the new ones. I wore a bed gown, so they just lifted my paralyzed arms and hands through its loose fit and let it rest on me. They didn't need to tie the cords at the back as I wasn't getting up any time soon.

I didn't mind my hands being crushed under me when I was changed or my internal organs slumping to one side because of the weakened muscle structure around them because I was just glad for the change of view. My mum had crammed full the only bit of wall to my left next to the window with postcards of Bible verses on them. They were very encouraging as they were themed around strength. But as they were behind me I could only see them once a day when I was changed. Their presence would provoke nurses into commenting, "I'm also a Christian, I'm praying for you."

Medications next, which were piped through my nose from a nurse's syringe. It took about 15 minutes to do all mine – I had a lot. After this, the therapists started arriving, briskly saying 'Morning' to the staff they passed in the corridor. They wore thicker and thicker coats, then gloves, and hats, as it got deeper into winter. They were passing by our entrance on their way to their offices only to all re-appear like ants at about 9ish to work with the patients. Wondering whether they would come to me for some kind of activity was the second most exciting part of my day. Of course, the most exciting part of the day was Sam's arrival.

Regular as clockwork when therapists approached, Screaming Lady would start. "Help me! Please help me! Aaargghhh! No. Go away! I beg you, please help me!" Her scream was a blood curdling, guttural cry coming from the ladies' room on the ward. Without fail it drew forlorn expressions from the nurses. I could hear them muttering forlornly under their breath to each other, "What else can we do? We've tried everything." I mean, I was in a bad way, a seemingly hopeless stroke condition to the naked eye, but even I was glad I didn't have that torment.

People Watching

The patients in my room had their own issues from different types of strokes. Opposite from me was Dribbly Starer. He was an eighty-year-old man of Afro-Caribbean descent. He dribbled A LOT, so much so that even I could see. The nurses and his family took turns to wipe his mouth. He didn't eat or talk so I don't know how he generated so much saliva. Propped up by all the spare pillows in southeast London, he just used to stare through me all day.

Diagonally across to my right was another Afro-Caribbean elderly gentleman. In a previous life he must have been an escape artist. He kept trying to find ingenious ways to slide out of his bed from under his sheets five or six times a day. This was no accident; he was definitely trying. But Burping Escapee was never going to escape because his constant burping would give him away. He burped as much as Dribbly Starer dribbled. Sam, Sophie, and Samuel tried not to laugh but failed miserably, whereas I was very good – I didn't move a muscle.

Next to me was an Asian guy in his fifties at first. He was unresponsive and his curtains were always drawn. His wife darted in and out of view occasionally. Unfortunately one day I got a very good view. His wife and a consultant went off to a side room and a few minutes later they came back sombrely. She was closer to my view than normal and obviously unaware I could see and hear everything. She turned to the consultant and said "Thanks for all you've done. I must say I was expecting it." With that, the nurses moved him in his bed to a side room where he died a few days later.

The bay was only empty for a day or so before Mr Belvedere arrived. He was in his sixties and could stand, talk, and eat, but not walk. He was wheeled to the loo and for his showers on a light blue seat on wheels – I'd love to have only been affected by my strokes like that. Being a local to me he knew of our church well. So, except for me, everyone was much older. Why was I so young having strokes? I thought strokes were only for old people.

The nurses were mainly the same age as me and were all very nice (except one). Computer Man who was very polite and efficient but seemed to love the corridor computer more than the patients. He only spoke to Sam, never to me. Then there were The Sisters. They were two bubbly, outgoing African Christian ladies who both lived very near to Belvedere. They took great honour in being able to care for a pastor. You couldn't *stop* them from talking at me. Trainee was a very young... trainee. I could tell Trainee was plucking up the courage to communicate with me over the weeks because she was noticeably staring when Sam and I communicated. I was convinced we'd communicate one day soon. Huff Puff was amusing. A small, stocky lady, she was very smiley but would huff and puff her way round her shift, sitting down at every opportunity, always verbally clock watching for the end of her shift. She used to talk out loud to herself like a mad woman as if we patients weren't there – very amusing.

There was a really softly spoken nurse who prefaced the start of every sentence with "Dave, I'm just going to…" whenever she was caring for me, and a very kind nurse who always bent down to my face close up telling me what, when, and why she was going to attend to me, but the exception was Bruiser. She should never have been allowed to be a nurse in my opinion. Rough and heavy handed with a Big Mama persona, my heart would sink when she came on shift. She was forever bruising my shins against the bed bars when she changed me. We had to complain about her in the end, which she didn't appreciate, blaming Sam for being bossy.

There were a couple of well-meaning chaplains. Being a 'vicar' (Baptist minister), it was assumed I would want a visit. Only I didn't really because I was listening in prayer a lot (let's face it, I had the time). They were quite traditional in their ministry whereas I'm more casual. They'd pull out their religious book that told them what to say, utter a few written prayers, smile, and walk on. But to be fair, I'm not sure what I'd have done when faced with someone in my position that I didn't know. Certainly, no religious book though.

The whole ward had a cleaner, Wipey, of African descent who silently came every day, wiping her mop around my bed as if I weren't there. But when she worked out from the Bible verses on the wall that I must have some sort of faith, you couldn't keep her quiet. She would hum songs I knew, then when she was told by the other nurses that I was a pastor it was "Hi Pastor Dave, how are you?" Blink. "Good."

Foodie, the meal lady, used to make me ponder my situation. All she did was come round every morning and take my neighbour's meal requests. She would read out some lovely options: toast, various jams, meats, veg, pastas, desserts, sponges, etc. Then she'd turn to me, check her list, look above my head (I guess it said 'Nil-by-mouth'), tick her sheet and then seemed to always pause for a bit and stare at me, probably wondering about my condition "Our friend doesn't eat" Mr Belvedere would remind her most days, "He's nil by mouth."

I 'ate' what I affectionately called 'burger sauce.' Not being able to move my jaw or swallow, I was fed through a tube in my nose. It looked gross but had all the dietary requirements I needed. I would catch glimpses of it in plastic bottles as the nurses fixed me up for a feed. It was orange in colour and had small green lumps in it and looked unappetising compared to next door's feast. So, I imagined it was Big Mac sauce instead.

Even though I only had burger sauce I needed laxatives which gave me constant tummy pain. When you're paralysed on the 'outside' you are affected on the inside as well. I was just too weak to soil my nappy and needed help. I thought at first it was a psychological block about not wanting to go to toilet in bed, but I was ignorant about the effects of paralysis and of lying flat for so long. Having a nappy was bad – not nice at all. Just like realising I had a catheter, needing a nappy was a constant reminder that I couldn't get up, walk, or have any privacy.

There were consultants doing their rounds every few days, always a junior doctor by their side with a laptop on wheels, furiously taking notes of their conversations with us. Not the most personable of touches, but necessary all the same. When they came round, having just come off life support, they would need to check my breathing. "Deep breath" they'd request, as they moved their stethoscope around my chest – but I couldn't. That became another regular reminder of how bad I was too. As was the fatigue I was suffering. Sometimes I'd just drift off to sleep while they were talking to me, apparently this is normal for stroke patients because the brain is working hard to reconnect with the limbs. I've experienced tiredness after a cycle ride or after a run, but never because my brain was working overtime. When it happened it developed in me an attitude of 'it's not my fault,' which was true, but a blessed relief because as a minister it's always my fault, especially when it's someone else's!

Butterflies

From the minute my eyes opened each morning I'd be waiting for Sam's arrival. By 10am I'd have butterflies because I knew she would be here any minute. My eyes would dart back and forth between the clock hands and the internal glass windows of the ward corridor she'd come down.

She normally arrived between 10:30am and 11am, but there was a chance that Samuel would get off to school early and she'd get a flyer through rush hour and, if a parking space presented itself on her arrival, she could be with me by 10 o'clock. I'd try and doze between 10am and when she arrived to speed things up, but I had too many butterflies – they hadn't been paralysed. I always got butterflies as a teenager cycling round to see her just as I would twenty-six years later waiting for her to come through the door after work at Belvedere.

On occasion after 10:30am, I'd have to battle negative thoughts that she might have had a car crash. Was she in hospital? What would that mean for Samuel? But right thinking would prevail because we were being divinely held, cradled even, and so were in good hands.

"Morning Sam" I'd hear multiple nurses cheerily say. I knew she was here, walking briskly down the corridor. She would appear any minute… and then there she was. Her smile would light up the ward every morning. With her long dark hair swinging side-to-side she'd bounce through the entrance on her ballet trained feet. She was a sight for sore eyes.

She would always read out to me all the social media messages she was getting, the hilarious emails from my cousin Richard – all of these communications were such a source of encouragement to us both and made me aware of just how many people I was going to have to thank, especially at church. They organised evening meals for the family every Thursday. I wasn't surprised by this because the level of love they had was off the charts: for the homeless, the debt-laden, for those out of work, the sick, for the elderly, for the community.

One Thursday evening, when the food was delivered Sam was asked, "Will David be back for Christmas?" Trying to get the message across about the seriousness of my condition was difficult because it was hard to comprehend, after all, some people are back to work a few weeks after their stroke. This church member wasn't alone in trying to compute the gravity of what had happened to me. "I had to read this more than a couple of times to take it in," was how many had responded to Sam's first social media update.

Sam quickly worked out early on that I would get achy from being paralysed. I needed to be regularly moved because of the danger of bed sores. Having laid completely still now for over a month, day and night, I was stiff. Just raising each knee for 15 minutes at a time was a great relief. Eventually she didn't even bother to ask if I wanted it, she just did it.

She'd busy herself by doing a bit of grooming for me – except shaving. She was too scared to do that so left it to my dad and Dom, my sister-in-law's husband. Her diligence and her daily devoted visits drew high praise from the nurses. These visits were made possible, of course, by her boss. I already held this lady in high regard because of how Sam had often spoken about her, but to give Sam literally 'all the time you need' was a massive weight off our minds - something we'd not take for granted. Her boss realised instantly from Sam's description that this was not your average stroke. I'd had four strokes and was expected to die, and if I survived not to have any quality of life – I was doing well just to be 'locked-in.'

At lunch time I would have a doze and Sam would need a change of scenery and time just to unwind. She knew I wasn't in pain; one knee was up, and I was being overcome by fatigue so she could have a worry-free hour just to herself over a muffin and a magazine. A bit of sanity amongst the numbing shock she and the family were in.

I wanted Sam to arrive earlier and leave later, she was the best nurse. I'd count the minutes till she came again the next morning. Sometimes when she left to get back for Samuel by school closing I would cry. I would never normally cry when she went somewhere. Given the circumstances you might imagine that I would cry, but this was not about that, it wasn't normal crying. I would feel normal levels of sadness inside, but insane levels of emotions would be uncontrollably expressed. Not only was something up with my temperature regulation, eyesight, and right-side hearing, but I was also discovering something was going on with my emotions. I'd have to find out what was happening somehow.

In case you're wondering how we managed to communicate about some of these struggles, we just talked about it. All we did was talk but not in the usual way…

Five

Blink... Blink, Blink

Once we knew my situation had stabilised we started to communicate about things outside of my condition. The meaning of it all, future accommodation, the kids' education, daily life – everything. Our communications were random, jumping back and forth as our minds whirred. But communication wasn't easy at first using an alphabet board because blinking out short sentences and Sam writing things down meant it was tediously slow.

On arrival, Sam had a bit of a routine going with me before we started communicating. First a kiss on the lips (I couldn't kiss back), then she'd always start the visit with these types of closed questions: Are you in pain? Are you comfortable? Are you hot? Did you have a good night? I could quickly blink once for 'Yes' or twice for 'No.' Then for the rest of the day, we'd just communicate using the alphabet board like we were normally chatting in a coffee shop, or on the sofa together with our knees touching.

We'd communicate about anything and everything. Soon she mastered the alphabet board quickly through regularity of use. She stuck her own board on the wall above my head so her eyes could dart back and forth easily between my eyes and the letters. She'd hold my board in one hand and a diary in the other, and a quick glance down at it from me would mean I needed reminding what I had said. The indication I wanted to start the conversation was me darting my eyes around the room, meaning 'Where is the board? I want to say something.' I would think of so many things overnight that when Sam arrived it would be like opening floodgates. Our families mastered using the alphabet board too and we were all praised by the nurses for our patience communicating this way, but to be honest it was a necessity.

Looking back now over Sam's jottings is very revealing. The alphabet board was in capital letters so the sentences below that Sam recorded I'd communicated in those early weeks are also in capitals, but there's no full-stops because we didn't have any.

Blinking Conversations

WHOSEGOTITWORSEMEORYOU This is how Sam started to jot things down, exactly as I was blinking them. But very soon due to the jumbled nature of the sentence she started asking me, "Is that the end of the word?" Blink or Blink, Blink. She'd have to work out my abbreviations too – "Is it 'I'm?'" Blink. If the answers to any of her questions were Blink, Blink she'd just try again. If any of this confuses you, imagine how we felt at first.

Occasionally she'd try to finish my sentences to speed communication up which would have been annoying at any time let alone now. It could take a few minutes to get a sentence worked out and any guessing or mistakes (worked out, apologised for, and started again) could set us back a few minutes so we found it best not to make them in the first place.

Anyway, back to the sentence, WHOSE GOT IT WORSE ME OR YOU. Finding out what had happened from Sam the night of the brain stem stroke, imagining what she had seen and heard and discovered from her own research, and now what she was handling every day, I thought she had it worse. I was just sedated or calmly lying down all the time.

I thought about the kids reaction to events and knowing they'd be looking to Mum to hold them together when her own world was falling apart. You tell me? Did I have it worse or did she? Sam told me the brain stem stroke I'd had was medically classed as a 'devastating' one. Worse than a 'massive' stroke, this wave that overwhelmed me was like a devastating tsunami. Overnight my body had been obliterated to absolutely nothing and my job, my house, my plans, and my life had all been left devasted in its wake. And not just me but my family too were devastated by its unstoppable force. They were completely up-ended; Sophie considering walking down the aisle someday without her dad; Samuel at his tender age no longer being assured of my approval; my church having their pastor dramatically swept away from them; my parents watching helplessly as their son lay helpless in its aftermath; the list of post-tsunami tidal surges just went on and on.

IM NOT LOCKED IN Sam found out that having locked-in syndrome meant someone is totally paralysed and only able to blink. They cannot swallow, smile, speak or feel anything anywhere and need life support to breathe because even their diaphragm doesn't work. They are literally locked-in their own body whilst fully cognitive.

However, there was very little information about people coming out of it. Then reality hit her... people don't come out of it. There is no known cure. They either die soon, or remain trapped in a world of misery, watching life pass by from the side-lines. There were literally two stories she could find about people coming out of it in our lifetime... in the whole world. There may have been more that she didn't know about, but in our age of medical research and communications, for a tech savvy person like Sam to only be able to find two cases was ominous for her.

She didn't want to tell me at first for fear of what it might do to my mental state, but our marriage was built on full disclosure and wasn't about to change. She needn't have worried though because that phrase I'd heard in intensive care before I even opened my eyes bubbled around inside me like a life-giving brook.

Each daunting new piece of medical information I learned about my situation just couldn't stop it bubbling around inside me.

This was not denial but just how it was. This allowed me to adopt two mindsets that you might not expect a person with locked-in syndrome to have. Firstly, because I loved all forms of communication and expression, this situation was interesting; and secondly, we used the alphabet board so much that I felt like my voice was getting heard and it made me think as though I wasn't locked-in. But if I hadn't heard The Voice, where would I be? What agony, what turmoil and distress to have locked-in syndrome suddenly foisted upon oneself. To this day I'm not sure how I would have coped.

NOW THEY'LL REALLY LISTEN When I used to listen to sermons in church the most powerful ones that really changed me as a person were those where I realised the speaker knew exactly what they were talking about. They had personal experience that illustrated their point. Up till now I had that about the message of mercy to a certain extent, but nothing as compelling as what was now happening to me. I never dreamed I'd be the living embodiment of the message. I could have preached a good sermon on mercy and how God helps us in our helplessness, but now I was experiencing it to an extreme extent. Though it may be hard to believe, I was lying there pulsating with purpose about preaching again.

IM ALL THERE I knew Sam needed to know how I was. Mentally everything was working. Cognition, memories, sense of humour, the lot. I was in my right mind. The whole family had got a glimpse of this when I had first asked if Lewis Hamilton had won the F1 World Championship. I had grown up watching F1 on Sunday afternoons with Dad and Stuart. Apparently, they laughed aloud when the therapists had enquired about what I had first communicated. Ignorant of the severity of my condition, I had just wanted to know the result of the race. Instead I should have maybe said IM ALIVE I LOVE YOU to the family. But I'd inadvertently given them hope. "That's my David!" I'm told Dad exclaimed. Typical of me at family gatherings to cut through the moment with inappropriate humour to lighten the mood. A character trait so often scorned had never been so welcome.

I WONT BE LIKE THIS FOREVER Sitting on my right-side level with my mid riff, Sam clasped my hands and sobbed whilst resting her head on my hip. She wanted to believe my words, but she also didn't want to get her hopes up, understandably. The consultant at St George's had to tell her some terrible things, and she'd had to make impossibly hard on-the-spot decisions. Like you, I can only imagine how hard that must have been. There were those two cases in the world in our lifetime where a near full recovery had been made, but that wasn't enough to give Sam certainty. Sam hadn't had a divine memo like me so her journey to faith was different. I was trying to reassure her.

I DO NOT TAKE COMMUNICATION FOR GRANTED I loved preaching and delivering hope, seeing people's expressions light up when they grasped the point. Hand gestures, voice inflections, dramatic pauses and poses to help make my point – that was my life up until then. I had come to the place where I could honestly say I didn't take any of it for granted. Given my condition, I was one of the few people in the world at that time who could think this and genuinely mean it without sounding pompously self-righteous – except I couldn't make any sound.

FEELS LIKE A TONNE WEIGHT Both Sam and our families were ravenous for information from me on what I was going through, and I was happy to share. It felt like I'd been pinned down under the collapsed rubble of a concrete building. I couldn't even breathe because the 'concrete slabs' (my muscles) felt so heavy. The brain stem stroke had sapped all my strength. I'd try and summon up all the effort I could and lift my arm or leg but couldn't, and nor could I feel myself trying. My brain just simply wasn't connected to any part of my body, except my vital organs and eyelids. I wasn't worried by this though and just processed it and accepted it as a present but passing reality.

ITS WEIRD HAVING A STROKE I never anticipated the purpose of my life being wrapped up with surviving four strokes, I was struggling to get my mind fully round it. I always knew something divine was supposed to happen through my ministry, but I never thought it would happen *in* me and *to* me. I could see how things were coming together and how events in my life were now making sense, but I always assumed that a good outcome (fulfilling your life's purpose) would come about by a good input, not a bad input. My expectations about my recovery were sky high and this unfolding plan impressed me no end.

FRONT COVER I was thinking ahead now to when I would preach again. I wanted to have my book cover done whilst in hospital so I could distribute it when I eventually preached. Sam's sister Sharon is a freelance magazine designer, and she was designing it. Inappropriate at that time I know, but that's just how I was thinking.

TAX RETURN It wasn't all contemplation about my future ministry but was entirely practical sometimes. It was the last thing Sam needed but it had to be done, and I'd be dishonest if I didn't say there was a small part of me that was glad I didn't have to do it.

WILL WE GO TO CYPRUS – this sounds crazy now, but I did genuinely ask this. I didn't know what to expect about my recovery at this point in terms of time. We were scheduled to go in July 2020. Apart from my strokes what else could possibly happen in the world that would threaten our going to Cyprus?

BUY A HOUSE Being a Baptist minister, most churches have a house for you to live in. I knew we'd be leaving Belvedere so would need a home of our own again. Sam had also started to think about our housing issue but hadn't broached it with me. When I said this, it unleashed a torrent of questions and thoughts, not least how she'd be able to manage it by herself with daily hospital visits going on. It was going to stretch her capacity even more on top of what she was already handling, and she was keenly aware of it too. But what choice did she have? We had to live somewhere, and we weren't going to rent and see how things panned out whilst our savings whittled away.

Sam knew only one place she wanted to be, and I agreed. She needed to be near family for future support for us both and that meant only one thing – our beloved home county of Surrey. In my experience, if Sam sets her mind to something she gets it. Whether a car, a holiday, or a house, she just has the knack. She'd have to find and develop a bargain property for five of us (Sam's dad was discovering it was too much for him to live alone so we had agreed pre-strokes he could live with us) and even then she'd have no budget to develop it because houses in Surrey don't come cheap. We'd also need a bigger deposit than we had because we were down my salary and couldn't borrow as much. ASK DAD AND STUART that was my answer. She was going to have to ask for help, but Sam was not used to that, so I communicated to them instead. Being a screenwriter and director, Stuart wasn't short of a bob or two, and Dad told me he'd been saving for a rainy day all his life - "Now is that rainy day" he said. 'Clever man' I thought. Without a moment's hesitation they both agreed to help along with Sam's dad too.

YOU'RE A SPECIAL LADY If you think what Sam was
mentally carrying at that time then add to that she was going to
have to relocate the family whilst effectively being a single parent
and renovate a house all by herself and eventually start work again,
you'd probably say the same thing. Her capacity to manage stress
and show deep devotion to me at the same time was being
stretched to the ultimate limit.

DO YOU NEED A BREAK ARE YOU SLEEPING I had to
check how she was. It was obvious for all to see that she was losing
a lot of weight. She never lost her smile though and she was
learning to accept offers of help. Being so organised and capable
she won't mind admitting she finds asking for or receiving help
quite difficult, but now our situation demanded that of her and I
couldn't keep asking for her. I heard how she'd asked the kids to
step up filling the void I'd left, and she willingly continued to
receive the wider family's continued help. She was sleeping at
nights now but refused my offer of taking a break from seeing me
every day. I was trying to relieve her of what could be nearly a
four-hour round trip each day. But she said communicating with
me about normal family matters gave her hope and that she
couldn't bear to be without me. The hour for lunch by herself in
our daily routine was just perfect for her. The weight loss stopped
after a few months so I could tell she was starting to 'breathe out'
a little.

SAMUEL NEEDS A DAD This made me cry when I
communicated this. I'd been suddenly taken from him, and he'd
been compelled to see things no fourteen-year-old should see,
right at the time when he was sprouting and starting his GCSE
years. He needed me more than ever. How was he supposed to
thrive at this time in his life when he could only communicate with
me through an alphabet board? The same was true of Sophie, she

had a new boyfriend which immediately made me feel a little lost. They were getting together just before all this happened. We wouldn't be able to share those daddy/daughter times we always had and that would inevitably be needed.

I'M SAD For one day I wasn't really communicative as I was so down processing everything, fleeting between what had been lost about our old lives and what somehow being 'okay' might look like for all of us. I just needed time to sulk about things, get it out of my system and go again. I needed time to adjust and mentally reposition myself to new prospects. SORRY FOR BEING NEGATIVE YESTERDAY IM HAPPY TODAY even when you're locked-in and paralysed, twenty-four hours and a good sleep makes a difference.

AFTER U GO ITS TOUGH Sam was the best nurse hovering round me like no nurse could, anticipating my every need. It was a long eighteen hours between her leaving and returning. After prayer there were just aches, pains, no human communication, boredom – just me, the goings on of my hospital room, and the unchanging view of the ceiling. It was like solitary confinement sometimes. But when Sam was there I felt a bit of normality again.

THAT'S MY GIRL/BOY During my times of processing my predicament one of the things I'd reasoned was that I could use my normal phrases to set the kids at ease. This is one of the things I used to say to the kids. They would tell me about their week, and I could give them my approval… with my usual cheeky wink. But how else could I be a father to Sophie and Samuel whilst paralysed and locked-in? By saying GET A CAT for years they'd wanted a cat and so had Sam and I, but we lived on unsuitable roads. Now I knew the area where our new house was located it seemed like the right time. Their response was one of disbelief mixed with surprise that after all these years I'd finally agreed to their badgering.

Sensing a moment of opportunity Samuel asked, "Can I have a TV in my new bedroom?" YES (I'd held off for years because with his love of computer games I knew we'd never see him again). He couldn't believe it either. I had to let them know in small ways like this that I was still Dad. These concessions might be a tiny distraction from my current predicament and give them things to look forward to.

Unexpected and Unscheduled

There was the odd time when the family slipped up in this new method of communication – like when Mum accidently spoke on my behalf to a nurse once in front of me. She innocently thought she was being helpful, but I was fuming about it. She thought she knew what I would have thought about something the nurse was asking me about through Sam and without a thought casually answered them instead of letting me laboriously spell out my sentence - and the nurse listened to her! Sam put them both straight.

It was virtually impossible to get the nurses to use the alphabet board. I think because mine was such a rare condition they thought they wouldn't need to use it again in their career, though one of The Sisters did confess she was scared as well. They preferred 'open' or 'closed' questions needing only a 'Yes' or a 'No' from me. One nurse did try and use it once which I found hilarious. She held the alphabet board and started pointing at each letter spelling CAN I HELP YOU she could have just asked me because I wasn't deaf. She thought the alphabet board was for her. To compound the matter she then tried to put a pen in my hand so I could write her my answer. The pen just dropped out of my hand as my fingers and arm couldn't move, so she shrugged in resignation and just walked off. I should have been offended but I just found it funny. I hope she didn't feel too awkward.

One evening though when the family had gone home, Trainee eventually plucked up the courage to communicate with me. She pulled up a chair by my bedside, slid the curtain round a bit so she was out of view and said, "They won't teach me how to use an alphabet board at Uni because the need is so rare, but I've watched you and your wife chatting away so if it's alright do you mind if I have a go?" BLINK I was absolutely delighted - at last a nurse to communicate with. I could tell she had been watching us because she was pretty good for a first timer: YOU'RE GOOD AT THIS "Thank you" she said. We proceeded to communicate till the end of her shift about cool places in the world we'd been. Trying to communicate where the Turks and Caicos Islands are via an alphabet board was comical. She'd obviously flunked geography but would be a good speech and language therapist.

Because of these experiences we limited the number of visitors so as to avoid these awkward situations with communication arising. However, there was one unscheduled visit that took us by surprise. The family had gone home, and I was by myself again. A man who was really associated with Sam through her work with Christians Against Poverty showed up. I'd only met him once, and that briefly. He seemed to fumble about for words for a few minutes, left some crisp packets and fruit 'for other visitors,' then left. I suspect he was anticipating a polite conversation with a fellow minister who'd 'had a stroke' and show kindness in bringing me some snacks. I don't think he was expecting to find me quite like I was. I hope he was alright.

Planned visits when Sam was around were different. A good friend of mine called Julian was invited along. He was a Spurs fan and they'd just surprisingly got a new manager that week, so I knew if I said his foreign name (which Sam neither knew nor could pronounce) he'd have plenty to say: MOURINHO True to form, off he went. My Baptist area minister visited. She was a literal Godsend. She put our minds at rest about a number of admin issues and explained how best to go about the move. The Baptist Union of Great Britain were very supportive and financially solved a few potential headaches, very generously Sam and I thought. All the arranged visits had gone so well that when Clive visited with his wife Jane, Sam left them with the alphabet board. They both had a go at experiencing the unique situation and were very good for first timers after Sam's tutorial. In the same vein Mick and his wife Wendy, who helped me, and others lead Belvedere Baptist Church, came up too. I expected a time full of their jokes and laughter and the visit did not disappoint.

There was one unexpected but pleasant 'coincidental' visit that occurred though. One morning a social worker appeared to see Mr Belvedere. The thing was I knew him. I knew him as a worker for a homeless charity, but he obviously had two jobs. For the past year I'd been working with him to steer a homeless drunk off the streets and into accommodation, and everything else that goes with that. It was that homeless man I'd been with in Accident and Emergency the day before my strokes. I was concerned that to this social worker and homeless man, I'd just fallen off the face of the earth in terms of contact. I wasn't concerned for my reputation, but for how the homeless man would feel. One of his issues was being let down by people. I KNOW THAT MAN I said to Sam. GET HIS ATTENTION Sam politely interrupted and explained who she was and what was going on. His face dropped, then looked flabbergasted. He came over to me "Hi David." 'What does he say in his position?' I thought. "So good to see you. I'll tell ..... (the homeless man's name) I've seen you. Keep getting better." He turned and left to carry on his social work. I was so relieved. If ever there was such a thing as Divine coincidence, that was it.

After the odd understandable slip up at the beginning with the alphabet board all members of our families got used to using it. Their visits became positively casual on Saturday afternoons at 3pm. SCORES There was a weird sense that normal service had resumed when I would ask about football. Stuart and Dad were equally as interested to know as I was – so between three and five o'clock I only had to blink SC for either of them to understand.

Mid-week though they couldn't come so much so I'd have to ask Sam about the European games which is laughable because she knows nothing and cares nothing about football. I had to spell phonetically to help her pronunciation and my understanding, BIYERN MUNIK I'd have to communicate (it reads Bayern Munich).

My wife's sister and her family came quite regularly to see me. Like my family we'd never seen them so much – work commitments being the usual culprit. But the situation was bringing us closer together and we shared some rather touching moments. One such moment was when Dom, my sister-in-law's husband, shaved my beard off. I never had a beard or even a five o'clock shadow, but I'd not been shaved for nearly a couple of months by this point. He travelled all the way over from one side of London to the other after a usual long day, on packed public transport, and got to me just after 6pm. A quick shave as he'd promised, a little polite chat on the alphabet board, then he had to leg it home and cook the family dinner. All told, a roughly two-hour journey for a five-minute shave. The next morning seeing my beard had gone, Sam asked if he'd done it. Blink DOMS A LEGEND.

Even Vicars Get Annoyed

It had been a long midweek day and Sam was struggling to write down what I was communicating. The situation wasn't helped by her being in a rush to get back for Samuel. I'd tried to say the same thing three or four times and she just wasn't getting it. I was annoyed and got frustrated rolling my eyeballs, which was the only way I could show it. I started breathing fast, tears streaming down my face. 'This is really difficult,' I thought, 'such a bad situation.' The awkwardness of it all was getting to me.

All the difficulties filled my mind: The length of time it took to communicate, the incorrect guessing by others about what I meant, then other stuff bundled in – having a nappy changed at aged forty-six, missing my kids growing up, being in hospital. What little breath I could muster was subtly panted out, my face went red, and tears appeared. "David, David, it's okay, it's okay. It's perfectly understandable." A soft hand touched my face and wiped away my tears. It helpfully distracted me out of that train of thought.

The hand had been that of one of The Sisters, usually jovial she spoke gently this time. What a great nurse, she calmed me right down. Sam gathered herself too, a bit blind-sided by my sudden, silent outburst. We agreed I needed a sleep and she needed to get ahead of the London evening rush hour traffic. We'd reconvene the next day when we were rested.

That same Sister was also running my room one night shift when a very embarrassing incident happened which could have been circumvented if she'd just used the alphabet board. I'll just say a somewhat pungent smell filled the room at about 3am – it was me. It took about forty-five minutes for the nurse to do her rounds in our room. She smelt it straight away and got a fellow nurse and started searching for the source. She started looking by a process of elimination out loud. "It can't be David; he needs laxatives and hasn't had any." But I'd seen my body convulse and put two and two together. She then proceeded to eliminate the other two men opposite as possible sources by waking and changing them. She woke my neighbour opposite and politely asked him, "No!" He wasn't best pleased. "That means it must be David. Is it you?" Now the whole room was going to find out. She looked at my eyes in desperation BLINK.

I think I was most annoyed by Wipey's spontaneous physio session. Now she knew I was a pastor I became her new best friend. I could see she would pat my left hand or arm most days, give her customary "Praise the Lord!" then clean round my bed while she broke out into song. This particular day Wipey obviously found a new sense of freedom and picked up my left arm. My left hand was a tight claw as a result of the strokes, so she pulled open each finger and slipped hers between mine. Agony! She noticed my arm was also tight so started to rub it. I was now alarmed but could do absolutely nothing except BLINK BLINK BLINK BLINK BLINK BLINK for no, no, no! But she wasn't a trained professional and didn't know that I was communicating. "They're going to give you physio…" pulling my arm up to the ceiling – Aaargghhh! Absolute agony. My left arm had been completely static now for about a month and it was as stiff as a door post. "…and you're going to start getting better." 'Not like this,' I thought. She then proceeded to push my arm up and down like a car jack. I was crying in pain. Thankfully, she stopped after a few goes and went about her business. My arm was throbbing.

In the morning when I was communicating to a horrified Sam what had happened, a consultant popped in and asked how I was. Sam firmly but politely relayed the situation to her. In sheer disbelief that Wipey had done this the consultant blurted out "I'm sure there's been a misunderstanding. I mean, how do you know she was a cleaner?" I darted my eyes furiously around the room to indicate to Sam that I wanted to communicate, indignant that I was not being believed yet seeing the funny side: SHE WAS HOLDING A MOP.

Drowning

There was one thing though that peppered all these daily communications – the necessary but dreaded suctions. They happened about six to eight times a day and four to six times a night. Because I couldn't swallow my saliva would build up in my airways making it harder and harder to breathe. This was obvious to all around as it would sound like I was breathing through water and felt like I was drowning – not pleasant and decidedly disconcerting. More than a few times Mr Belvedere would shout for assistance, "Our friend sounds like he needs help with breathing!" If it were night-time I'd have to wait till a nurse would walk past and hear my loud gargling, no wonder I hated nights. But during the day family members would draw the attention of the few specially trained nurses who could perform a suction.

They would send any visitors out of my bay, pull the curtains round, and suck the saliva out of my airways. They held a thin plastic flexible tube connected to a pump behind my head and would insert it into a tube cut in my neck through a procedure known as a tracheostomy. My nose and mouth were bypassed by this tube called a trachea and it made me feel vulnerable knowing I was breathing only through a small tube.

When the suction began my whole body would vibrate as the muscles had no strength to control themselves. The process would cause me to wrench to the right and my left hand would violently vibrate out of control looking like it had been electrocuted. The suction would prompt a huge series of coughs which also helped to eject the saliva. Nurses would often say, "Oh, you've got a strong cough there. That's good." It didn't hurt but was extremely uncomfortable. The bodily reactions would cease when they pulled out the thin flexible plastic tube from my throat. It would only last about ten seconds, but sometimes they'd have to go in again to fully clear the airways. Not a sight for anyone to see, except Sam (though I did let Sophie and Samuel see once as I felt they needed to know what I was going through). At times I was ambivalent to how uncomfortable the suctions were due to their frequency, but at other times they would really get me down.

Once by mistake there was no specially trained nurse available to give me a suction. A calm panic descended on us all including scurrying nurses looking for one, until they found one two hours later. My chest was heavy, and my gargled breathing was loud. It was the closest I ever want to come again to drowning in my own saliva.

Fortunately, there was some serious consolation about to be realised. It had been creeping up on me since my first night in Lewisham without me realising its significance...

Six

Breakthrough!

It was a winter's morning like any other, Sam had arrived, and the consultants were doing their usual rounds. He wanted to do a 'touch test' with me to test my feeling. He proceeded to prod me, "Do you feel that?" Blink. On a different limb he'd prod me again, "Do you feel that?" Blink. He went on around my limbs and lastly said, "Do you feel that?" BLINK BLINK "That's good, I didn't prod you then. I suddenly realised what had happened and darted my eyes around the room. I FEEL EVERYTHING EVERYWHERE What a breakthrough! The aches, the pain of Wipey's impromptu physio session, the soft hand of one of The Sisters on my face, no more floating – feeling had returned everywhere, and I hadn't realised it until now. "Hmm… that's a very good sign for potential recovery" he said.

The consultant's confirmation of my sensations was a moment of gratifying satisfaction for me because my expectations were starting to be met. My recovery had started, and the medical profession was catching up with the fact. Calm yet surprised, he said that there can be a permanent loss of feeling in some limbs when you have a brain stem stroke as devastating as mine. Hope was starting to build for Sam; first I'd survived, then I'd come off life support and now this. Something was starting to happen in me that was beyond both of us. The nurses who overheard knew it too; I could tell because they were going about their business close by with smiles.

Dominoes

Things just began to happen like a trail of dominoes falling down. To the joy of The Sisters and the surprise of the consultants, my right foot just 'woke up' perfectly days after this test. I suddenly became able to flick my ankle in all directions and wiggle my toes like nothing had ever happened to it. Next, my right leg gingerly became able to bend a bit. Other areas of my body were more subtle (we're talking millimetres here). Sam documented in her diary on the 26th of November that I did a tiny smile in the left corner of my mouth when she greeted me. I could only subtly twitch my quad muscles in my left leg, but it was movement all the same.

"How did you know you could move it (the right ankle)?" Stuart asked. IT FELT LIGHT Previous to this I'd felt severe heaviness all over, so when it lifted off my right ankle, out of curiosity I tried to wiggle it. A part of me felt free. "Why do you keep wriggling your right foot?" Dad asked BECAUSE I CAN I'd been completely paralysed for nearly a month – you bet I was going to move it.

About the same time I became able to lift my right forearm a few millimetres off the bedsheets from the elbow and the right fingers started to gingerly respond to my waggling. My right hand felt like pins and needles that didn't hurt. I remember thinking then, 'So this is how you come out of paralysis; slowly and with strange sensations.'

At the end of that first month I caught myself doing a random swallow. I hadn't tried, the throat muscles sensed the saliva dripping down my airways and dealt with them accordingly. I WILL GET BETTER, I reinforced to Sam. She smiled this time with hope returning in her eyes because little by little every physical milestone that was happening to my body was chipping away at the doubts sown in her mind after that first harrowing week.

She was in a weird kind of suspended animation I thought; being told one thing, seeing another, hoping for the best but not wanting to be ignorant of the facts whilst reading encouraging verses from the Bible. After twenty-six years of marriage I knew Sam wasn't an early adopter, though not a late bloomer either. She was in the middle like a lot of people. But once she was convinced she was unswerving in her convictions.

Nothing much else seemed to be happening with my left side, so just for a laugh one day, Samuel picked up my left hand carefully and prized my fingers open (they were in a tightly clenched fist all the time) and put them around his. "Hey Dad, let's do an arm wrestle." We used to do that a lot at the dining room table. He was never going to win being young, but now he was starting to sprout in height and strength and with me at my weakest, this was his chance. He just put a little tension in his arm as he was being careful not to hurt me like Wipey. I put everything I had into it not even knowing if my left arm would respond because it still felt heavy. My triceps responded and I slowly pushed his arm down in stuttering fashion. "Woah!" exclaimed Sam and Samuel in unison. I was surprised too. We did it a few more times till Samuel found the point of tension that held both mine and his arm in equilibrium. "Dad, that's good." It was really weak and stiff, but we were all encouraged.

In early December you could tell how Sam was feeling about my progress because in her social media update she used the phrase 'when he can eventually come home.' Her updates were a vital source of encouragement to those praying and wishing us all well, but she just couldn't keep up with the rate that things were happening to me. Soon after I started shrugging my right shoulder a little. It was so subtle that Sam had to touch it to feel what I was feeling. My left hand could manage a very subtle clench of a millimetre or so by now, and by mid-month I was using gravity to help my right hand touch my chest, albeit with the elbow seemingly welded to the mattress. A few days later I tried my first subtle wave with my right hand. The Sisters noticed and got really excited, sometimes just coming into the room to provoke me into a wave.

Weirdly, sneezing and hiccups returned. Not big things in themselves, but when put together with these other movements we were all clearly getting the picture that my body was 'waking up.' The hiccups were uncontrollable though, because of my severe diaphragm weakness. Since I could now feel everything everywhere that meant I could also feel itches. If you can't scratch an itch don't worry, they go away after about twenty seconds, but never had I been so glad to feel them.

There was also a big development in my use of the alphabet board. My neck started to gingerly respond to me wanting to move it slightly in all directions, so my Blink or Blink Blink gradually morphed into a mix of subtle nodding, shaking, and blinking. I was becoming like a toy drummer boy seriously low on batteries.

Neuroplasticity

On one of their weekly rounds a consultant said all this progress was down to 'neuroplasticity.' As I understood it from him my brain should be forming new neural pathways to reconnect it with the nervous system, making my limbs work again. Unfortunately, this doesn't happen for everyone but it was happening to me everywhere to a greater or lesser extent except to my left foot. What was interesting him was the speed and the plentiful nature of my signs of recovery despite the devastating nature of my brain stem stroke.

He was further interested because my thrombectomy had failed. I discovered it was a procedure I'd had whilst unconscious to try and remove the blood clot and eliminate the fatal danger of blood swelling on the brain. Not being able to remove the clot meant the brain would have to work much harder reconnecting, thus severely hampering my chances of any recovery. I think that's why they told Sam I had very poor odds for survival and would be institutionalised if I survived. But my clot mercifully dissipated just with clot removing drugs.

To help neuroplasticity you're supposed to think the thoughts of reconnection, that your limbs are moving even when they're not. I tried that daily for weeks on my left foot especially, tapping it with my right foot and imagining it moving – why not? But it didn't work so I stopped. What did seem to be working for me was just trusting in "You're going to be okay." And before anyone admires such faith, I honestly felt like I didn't have a choice because those words kept bubbling away inside me. I never had any sense that I was fighting for my life, or fighting against the odds, rather it was as though I had a front row seat and was just calmly watching mercy unfold in me.

A Chance of Death

Soon the therapists started talking about getting the feeding tube removed from my nose and inserting a plastic tube directly into my stomach through the skin, called a peg. This standard procedure would take about fifteen minutes and be done under a little bit of sedation, called an endoscopy. It would remove the blur I had to my lower left vision as the bulge in my nose made by the tube would be gone. For everyone it represented the last tube out of my face.

With all operations there is a risk, so to put the kids at ease they were given an actual peg to hold and look at, and Sam and I had the risks downplayed to us in explanations. Finally, after three aborted attempts, I was to have the endoscopy done on the 16th of December.

Sam went home the night before after yet another good day of surprising progress. I was told I had to be 'nil by pipe' for the twenty-four-hours before the endoscopy. It was scheduled for early afternoon, so I was expecting no 'burger sauce' for the evening. But at around 6 o'clock Huff Puff huffed and puffed her way over to me with some burger sauce. It was her first of a few attempts to feed me to which I slowly shook my head because I was not going to have her mistake mess this fourth attempt up.

Huff Puff wouldn't use the alphabet board so phoned Sam about what to do. She came back a few minutes later and directly asked me, "Is it to do with the endoscopy tomorrow?" I smiled with the left corner of my mouth and nodded gingerly. "Oh, don't worry, you can have feed until midnight the night before." 'Oh, that's okay then' I thought. So I let her rig up the feed. The next morning Sam came in looking a bit awkward but with a wry smile on her face. It turns out Huff Puff had said on the phone to her that I'd lost the will to live and wouldn't eat anymore. She even asked Sam to come back that night and plead with me to eat as they 'weren't getting through' to me. All because Huff Puff wouldn't use the alphabet board. Sam knew me too well and didn't believe her for one minute after the good day we'd had.

Miscommunication wasn't the only hurdle we had to get over. The other one was my locked jaw. It had been locked with only about one centimetre gap between my teeth since the night of the strokes. This hadn't bothered me up till now because I was breathing through my trachea and hadn't noticed it. I needed three centimetres gap for the child mouth guard to facilitate an internal camera used in the endoscopy. The experienced nurse who knew this worked out that wedging it in from the left side of my mouth made it possible – phew.

Whilst in the waiting bay for the endoscopy, a nurse came in and left a 'waiver' form for Sam to sign on my behalf. It spelled out the risks of the procedure and that all efforts would be taken to… prevent my death. Under normal circumstances most of us would just fill in the form and return it but bearing in mind I had succumbed to the miniscule chance of having four simultaneous strokes and being locked-in, it really raised my awareness. It was the first time in my life I'd had to consider the minute chances of death happening to me could actually be realistic. But it didn't seem rational to me to survive what I'd survived only for it all to be scuppered by an endoscopy and I certainly wasn't going to live the rest of my life as a hypochondriac. My faith was emboldened, and Sam signed the waiver for me.

Just as well the experienced nurse had come down with us for the procedure because the last thing I remember was the surgeon giving up with the child mouth guard and her taking over to try and force it in my mouth like we'd practised. The surgeon said it was a tricky operation and I wouldn't thank him the next morning when I woke up feeling I'd been 'kicked in the stomach by horses.' We were ecstatic though because all tubes and wires were now gone from my face. The surgeon was right about the pain in the end because it cost me an entire week of physio sessions.

Tranquillity

There'd been an initial assessment of me by the physiotherapy team no less than two weeks after the strokes. I still couldn't feel anything at this time. Three female physios hauled me up into a vertical sitting position on the edge of the bed. "I'm holding your back and the girls are holding your legs in place. If you start to fall back, left, or right I'll catch you and if you fall forward they'll push you back to me" the physio assured me. I could see my feet dangling and the two other girls crouching in front of me, hands up, hovering close to my shoulders.

I sagged like an unsupported vertical pillow. I couldn't hold myself. My gaze was straight down as I couldn't even lift my head at that point. I could hardly believe it was me seeing the girls correcting and supporting my limbs as I slumped this way and that, but not feeling anything. My body had been totally devastated right back to zero.

The lead physio for the ward had assigned herself to me. She saw me every few days because she and her small team also had three other rooms of four patients to help. She used to put her mousy brown hair up in a bun for work. She wore blue uniform trousers with a white blouse. She was a very tranquil person, bringing such calm to my bedside in all her sessions. Tranquillity had a lovely calm but authoritative voice which really put me at ease when she administered the dreaded suctions. I was always excited when she strode on to the ward because it might be my turn for some physio.

Things were different since the initial assessment now breakthroughs were happening; strength was returning in places. One morning Tranquillity cradled my lower right leg in her arm and pushed my knee up towards my chest. "Try and push me away, David." Wham! She had to steady herself. I'd put all my effort into it as usual – I didn't do ninety-nine percent. "Sam, you'd better feel this."

Sam moved round the bed and cradled my leg ready for me to push her away. Wham! "Woah!" she exclaimed. "You've got some good strength there, David," said Tranquillity. In similar fashion they both tried my left leg. Though not as dramatic it had a weaker but definite response.

I NEED PHYSIO EVERY DAY I'd tell Sam. I LOVE EXERCISE I would say. I couldn't get enough, not because I loved exercise per se but because it just got me moving. Lying paralysed in a bed 24/7 isn't good for anyone.

Legs and arms 'pushing away' movements were something the family helped me exploit. Each member of my family became a physio – Sam, Mum, Dad, Stuart, Mark, Sophie, and Samuel, for about five minutes at a time each. I was so keen I'd communicate to them to do it at least a couple of times a day when they were there. We didn't know it then but that was the start of my family playing a crucial role in my bodily recovery. Sometimes when they'd lift up my legs or arms for the exercise they'd encounter unexpected resistance. I AM ALWAYS RESISTING YOUR MOVEMENT I would explain. They were moving and stretching my limbs, but I turned it into strength training learned from my teenage years.

My family would massage my toes and fingers, arms and legs, anything to simulate movement and get the blood flowing. But they paid special attention to my left hand. When different family members were saying their goodbyes at the end of a visit I'd stare at my left hand. That motion would draw their attention to it, and they knew what I meant (that way was quicker than using the alphabet board). The hand was always clawed up like a tightly clenched fist so they would prize it open and press the top of the palm down into the pillow spreading the fingers. Shortly after they went any itch, sneeze or yawn would make it claw up again – but it was worth it for those few minutes of openness.

After thinking about the discovery of my leg power for a week or so, I wondered if I might be able to hold my weight. I WILL TRY TO STAND UP TODAY I communicated to Sam which she relayed to the physio team the next time they came. "No chance!"

they said, laughing it off. And for good reason; if I couldn't even balance myself on the edge of the bed a few weeks ago how was I to balance vertically and hold my weight? I was getting a bit ahead of myself, but I didn't know how things were supposed to go, never having come out of total paralysis before.

The one solitary wheelchair I'd seen in the corridor that first morning in Maple Ward was all we had between eighteen patients I was told. We had to take turns and now after six weeks, this morning it was my turn. Tranquillity had to secure me in a mobile hoist and lift me into it. It was a big black cumbersome chair with big wheels, wide armrests and a padded head rest with side panels around my temple area so my head wouldn't slump to one side. It had a soft padded seat and pillows were stuffed all around me and I was told I would have to learn to 'tolerate' it, whatever that meant. If I'd taken time to consider what I looked like in that chair with my trachea and oxygen tank secured (I was on two litres of oxygen per minute then) it would have got me down I'm sure, but from my viewpoint it was progress and that was positive.

It was just past 10am. 'Sam will be here soon, this'll surprise her' I thought. It was my first time since the strokes that I'd been out of bed. "David, wow! You're in a chair" she exclaimed as she appeared around the bay curtain. TAKE ME ROUND THE WHOLE WARD I communicated. Simply being wheeled around a room as opposed to lying still 24/7 staring at the ceiling was incredible, like life was starting again.

I saw the corridor she walked down every day, the side rooms for individual patients, Computer Man's ward computer he was surgically attached to, even the welcome desk at the very front of the ward. 'So this is what it's like being in a wheelchair' I thought. Everyone was saying 'Hi' as I was pushed by. I felt rude because all I could do was stare back in whichever direction the chair was pointing – it wasn't my fault. Being a church minister it's always your fault no matter what's happened and not to return a greeting from someone was a crime, but here they all understood my perspective for once and it was such a relief. How wonderful to be extended the grace just to be accepted as David, who can't turn his head or lift his right arm quick enough or even speak.

Sam brought me back to my bay. Tears were streaming down my eyes now, not because of the joyous new-found freedom of not being a judged minister, but because my backside was killing me. Laying in a bed with your weight spread all over your body for a few weeks to suddenly having it all go through your backside takes weeks to tolerate. 'Ah, that's what the physios meant.' It was just like getting seriously saddle sore from a new bicycle. Even so I was elated after my first excursion. THIS IS AMAZING.

Sprightly

The occupational therapist I had was very bubbly and smiley. She was great. Sprightly had adopted a typically British name that was easier to pronounce than her real Eastern European one. She had dyed blonde frizzy hair and used plenty of foundation make up. She wore the same white blouse as Tranquillity, but this time with green trousers. "Good morning, David. Would you like to do some personal care practice?" she'd say cheerily. Blink - why not?

Sprightly would come two or three times a week for the whole time I was there, teaching me to let her move my limbs to do simple grooming tasks for the sake of muscle memory. Moving the electronic bed up so I sat vertically she would helpfully explain in her endearing accent everything she was doing and why. They were good sessions which I always looked forward to. She put the hairbrush in my hand one session, and it fell straight out again as I couldn't hold it. My hand grip that The Sisters kept joyously making a fuss about was actually so weak it couldn't even hold a hairbrush. Sprightly clasped her hand round mine and completed the hair brushing attempt.

In our next session Sprightly asked me "Are you okay if I use a mirror this time? After a stroke people can be understandably hesitant to see the new 'them'." BLINK was my response. She held the mirror up and there I was. My hair was unkempt, a bit matted with no particular style. My right eye blinked slower than my left in an uncoordinated fashion. My right eyebrow was weirdly lower than the left and my lips were kind of pouted even though I wasn't trying. 'I look disabled' I thought. I saw my trachea for the first time too, 'I'm breathing through that' I reacted, 'Who'd have thought?' Even though I was distracted by the 'new physical me,' I felt the same positive, competitive Christian inside.

The session continued with other personal care mimicry, but as I could literally do nothing it was fairly short. My mind wasn't on it anyway. I pondered what I'd seen, 'Hmmm, suppose I'd better deal with it' I reasoned. 'That's physically the new me - for now.'

Deciding My Future

IM NOT GOING TO GET BETTER HERE I told Sam. The care I was receiving was wonderful, but they'll be the first to admit I needed more long-term care and daily 1:1 rehab. They weren't set up for that nor did they pretend that they were. I knew it and they knew it. I had no idea if such a place existed, but if I were to be 'okay' somewhere suitable would need to be found, I was sure of it.

Tranquillity and Sprightly were onto it and my family were onto it too. A few places were discussed offering different types of care. There was one they discovered which was only thirty minutes away from my parents in the county of Surrey called The Royal Hospital for Neuro-disability, Putney. Bizarrely, one night when my parents drove the kids up to see me in St George's, Sophie had already spotted it. The traffic came to a halt due to a crossing, the car now stationary directly outside the hospital entrance. Sophie pointed it out to everyone in the car and took a photo to remember it in case I would need it. Was she unknowingly divinely inspired?

My family started researching it after a meeting with nurses and therapists who recommended it and Stuart even paid a visit there and got a guided tour from the male lead physio. Stuart took a number of photos as he went round and showed them all to me recounting what Tour Guide had told him. It was a huge Victorian building with modern extensions and was a charity in its own right with part funding from the NHS. It used to be called 'The Home for Incurables' which sounded ominous. But when Stuart enthused about the recently refurbished rooms and the new sports hall-sized gym I was excited. I wasn't quite sure what I'd do in a gym since I couldn't even sit up, but everyone was convinced Putney offered the intensive rehab I needed. I was relieved such a place of intensive rehab existed. There was only one problem though: they had a huge waiting list. A patient on my ward had already been waiting three months with no sign of any movement.

As well as making plans for my future rehab we were also making plans where to live. We were communicating about Surrey county towns to live in. Soon enough Sam had found a bargain property in one close to our childhood village. It was a 1950's two-bedroomed bungalow that looked like it hadn't been touched since its construction. Our speciality - it was almost too good to be true. Sam would know exactly how to go about renovating it. It just confirmed what I'd heard from day dot about the outcome of my condition.

Aware of all Sam was juggling I said SAMUEL HELP RENOVATIONS He had helped me a bit with our flat in Sidcup the previous year that we'd developed, so now was the time for him to step up a bit. Sophie's input was going to be with the plans as she was studying to be an architect. Being five years older than Samuel she had experience with a number of our past renovations but wouldn't be around much because of university. Samuel needed to help Sam with the day-to-day stuff. It was a proud parent moment – I knew he'd take the initiative as the gravity of the situation was abundantly clear.

As Sophie got to work on the bungalow plans the therapists hatched their plan for me to jump the queue and get into Putney quickly. They had special single rooms for those like me who had a trachea. The therapists planned to try and get me ready to have the trachea out but leave it in so I could be admitted to Putney, and they could do the extraction soon after arrival. There seemed no time like the present to start the plan as Christmas was fast approaching. Surely any other breakthroughs would be reserved for Putney...

Seven

I Couldn't Say Goodbye

I have a lot to thank the speech and language profession for, as I do all the professions, but they were the ones to make a significant contribution to my quality of life right at the beginning. Their training me with the alphabet board was so good that our use and our family and friends use of it made me feel not locked-in. The profession was about to step up to the plate and perform again.

Politeness

The ward speech and language therapist would arrive sometimes before Sam arrived, sometimes when Sam was there, and sometimes when the whole family was there. She was very much involved with us and was greatly appreciated by all. She was tall, with a long ponytail, very polite and sharp with an accent from the Home Counties.

Politeness used to hover at the edge of the slightly drawn bay curtains wanting to be respectful of mine and Sam's visiting time together yet wanting to come in and do her speech and language session. But there was no need for Politeness to feel that way because we were a very welcoming couple. Borne out of years of church work, first with Clive and Jane, later our own community engagement projects then life as an ordained vicar, hospitality was our 'thing' – being locked-in wasn't going to change that. My eyes would dart back and forth between Sam and Politeness so Sam would get the hint someone else was there. All the therapists and nurses knew family involvement was a key to recovery, so Sam was always included in my sessions with Politeness.

Cuff Down

Tranquillity and Politeness worked together to realize their plan of getting me prepared for Putney by focussing on my swallowing, ready for the trachea to come out. This process was what they termed 'cuff down.' They would deflate the size of the little balloon (called the cuff) inside my throat that protected my lungs from my saliva. Over the remaining time I was in Lewisham they would judge how to do this for longer and longer periods of time each day, matching my brain's recovery of its control over swallowing. Their aim was to get to where the cuff could be down all the time, fully using my mouth and nose to breath normally.

They started with ten minutes trial first. Tranquillity would suction me first to clear the airways then Politeness deflated the cuff. I would feel the air fill my airways to the rear of my throat and nose. "Can you feel anything, David?" they would ask expectantly. THIS FEELS BRILLIANT Normality was what I craved and this, along with my right ankle having started moving perfectly, was exactly that. My eyesight was weird, my right ear muffled, I wasn't able to use my mouth, tongue, or swallow, nor could I take a deep breath still and I was pretty much paralysed. But for the first time since the strokes I was breathing in the normal way. But in my severely weakened state, the effort it took for my airway muscles to move air from my trachea to my nose would send me off to sleep often – that's how bad I was that I fell asleep exhausted after breathing a few breaths.

A few days later they also tried a speaking valve over my trachea at the same time, but I couldn't consciously move my voice box, so no sounds came out. I thought that words would automatically tumble out, but I quickly realised that my voice box was a muscle. I would have to wait for neuroplasticity to occur for my voice box to be reconnected with the brain. I remember thinking to myself a phrase I used to use when Samuel's youthful impatience would cause him to fret – 'poise.'

I wouldn't need poise for long though. I SWALLOW AT NIGHT this was involuntary initially, but I had started noticing it every so often. Politeness thought we should try a FEES test (a Fibreoptic Endoscopic Evaluation of Swallowing) which is where they shove a tiny camera up your nose and down your throat whilst they try and induce a swallow – yuk! They did that by using squirts of bitter lemon juice into my mouth to try and shock a swallow. It didn't work the first time, but I realised something significant had happened. I CAN TASTE AND SMELL IT A good thing had been discovered from the first failed attempt.

The very next day, Politeness caught me doing an involuntary swallow (I've never had someone so interested in my Adam's apple) and this was all the confirmation she needed to continue with lengthening the cuff down daily process. The only thing was that when my cuff was down I was prone to coughing fits because of saliva dripping into my lungs. This meant they would stop the cuff down process for that day, give me a suction and let me rest - which I didn't want of course. Anything would set me off: a joke, a surprise, too much activity, even Sam getting excited about some new progress I'd made. Such subtle movements in my neck were enough to trigger me off.

My cuff was usually let down before Sam arrived. As soon as she appeared I was always keen to communicate what had happened in my body since the previous day (because little bits of recovery seemed to be happening that fast and always at night), I'd have to preface everything with DON'T GET EXCITED BUT to avoid a coughing fit. She learned to suppress her joy pretty quickly, but it became a bit of a routine every morning: DONT GET EXCITED BUT MY MOUTH MOVES, DONT GET

EXCITED BUT MY LEFT LEG TWITCHES, DON'T GET
EXCITED BUT I TOOK A DEEP BREATH.

Apart from a few setbacks of coughing fits and pure tiredness,
the cuff down process proceeded smoothly. A few days before
Christmas I did a whole day 'cuff down.' By then I wasn't having
coughing fits at all and the need for suctioning was happily
reducing because of occasional swallows. Though still locked-in I
felt relaxed and encouraged by what was happening with my
throat. After this successful 'cuff down' day Politeness came to
review the situation with me, and we decided to leave the cuff
down permanently. 'Why not?' I thought. When Sam arrived I
communicated DON'T GET EXCITED BUT MY CUFF IS
DOWN PERMANENTLY NOW even though it didn't matter if
she did get excited. And there was me thinking any more
breakthroughs would be reserved for Putney. Our families adopted
that phrase to excitedly sum up my latest progress, like one
evening when my parents were getting packed up to leave I
overheard them chuckling to each other, "Don't get excited but…"
whilst recounting my progress since they'd last seen me.

The Most Wonderful Time of the Year?

Since about late November most radio stations were playing wall
to wall carols and Christmas songs and my radio, brought by my
younger brother Mark, was the de facto one for the room – blaring
into my left ear dawn till dusk. It had been nice the odd time at
first to have the radio on and get into the Christmas spirit, but now
we were in mid-December. What had been a wonderful idea of
Mark's had inadvertently turned into a nightmare. I was stuck – I
couldn't be all 'Bah humbug' and get the radio taken away by the
family and I definitely couldn't turn it off myself. But
communicating FORGET CHRISTMAS to Sam one day did come
across a bit 'Bah humbug.'

It wasn't because I was depressed about my condition, rather I didn't want Sam to worry about going to the extravagant lengths she went to every year to make the time of year so fabulous. Loads of drink, cake, presents, decorations, food, hospitality – she made Christmas for our family. She had enough on her plate juggling keeping sane for the kids, handling daily visits, running the house, and organising our future. I wanted her to feel she could dial it down a bit.

But she didn't take it on board totally. She got Sophie to bring in a small, fake Christmas tree and Samuel brought in the decorations. It became the room tree – a wonderful touch seeing as we only had a solitary stick-on-glass star put up by the staff. I WANT TINSEL I communicated. That was a big ask as tinsel had been banned from the house ever since we got married. I'd grown up with my mum's subtle use of it, but Sam had only ever seen it overused. "I think it looks tacky" Sam would always say. It became sarcastically known as one of those massive sacrifices I'd made to keep our marriage together - I'd been emotionally wounded all these years. When Samuel pulled out the tinsel there was much mockery. IS HAVING FOUR STROKES ALL I NEEDED TO DO TO GET TINSEL I communicated. Amongst the rather muted celebrations that was a truly wonderful moment.

Something not so wonderful though was missing our family's annual trip up to central London to see the Christmas lights with my cousin Richard and his family. This year we wouldn't be doing that. It was the first 'thing' that everyone couldn't do because of my strokes. It began to sink in how my strokes were affecting more than just me and my immediate family, but the activities of the wider family too.

It wasn't wonderful either when my brother Mark sank his head down on to my chest and started sobbing one night near

Christmas. He wasn't crying about my situation, but his own. Life was going on without me and something had really upset him. This was rare, he'd never do this. But because he'd just poured out his heart to his locked-in brother he'd felt listened to. All I wanted to do was hug my little brother back but I couldn't. It was a moment of new-found intimacy and a powerful lesson in listening I'll never forget. Being a minister could never teach me that as well as being locked-in could.

Christmas Day was definitely the most wonderful time of that year for me, considering the year I'd had. We had our usual family gatherings, albeit in a hospital around the foot of my bed. There was an unspoken permission to be joyful because of the signs of progress I was making, but the family was still tentative, wondering what our new future would look like.

At dawn that morning I remember thinking 'So, this is what it's like for all those people I pray for every year.' In my Christmas Day services I'd always prayed for those alone who were not experiencing a typical Christmas for whatever reason. I was not experiencing a typical Christmas Day at all, and I was alone in my own world, so I knew somewhere a Baptist pastor would be praying similar prayers I would be benefitting from.

Seeing my whole family later that morning and being able to communicate with them was good for the soul. I was communicating so much and cracking jokes a lot of the time. Each of family members rotated in their use of the alphabet board throughout the day. By that time I was starting to raise my neck and head a little, so I was able to get an individual's attention that way. As a gregarious and loud person, I was usually fairly central to everything going on at family gatherings, so it was a bit of a contrast this year being silent but still being central to things with everyone positioned around my bed. We used to have everyone round our house anyway because we always seemed to have the best suited house for a family gathering. This year everyone was round my 'house' again but for very different reasons. Come early evening, when they all left to have their own muted Christmas meals without me, I wasn't sad but fulfilled and exhausted. Then Boxing Day came, and we happily did it all again.

In terms of parties New Year's Eve was non-existent, but New Year's Day still had that similar feeling of expectancy about it as previous years when the family all met together again. How many 'Don't get excited but…' moments would there be going forward? How would the new house turn out? What new avenues of ministry might open up as I recovered? I was locked-in and mainly paralysed but couldn't stop being thankful for my survival, for my early signs of recovery, for Sam, my family around me, and how the house sale was going through in record time. From my perspective at that time, I just couldn't see a downside to my predicament.

New Year's Day also felt similar because we played 'The Bag Game' as usual, only this time with a little twist. Each New Year's Day Mum would fill twelve material bags each with a small household item. Then we'd have to feel the objects and write down our guesses. There were always score controversies at the end because the Hazeldine clan was very competitive. Of course I couldn't hold anything or write – but I could smell now. So this year Mum had small plastic pots with lids that had captured essences or had smelly objects in. It was a great way of including me. We all had to recognize the smells to much hilarity. I was rubbish and came last and there was no chance they would let me win out of sympathy.

When it came to Sophie's birthday a few days later however, I didn't feel so joyous. I just felt sorry for her having to do most of her celebrations in the hospital with me. And when she could celebrate with her friends, I knew she'd be thinking about me. I wanted her to celebrate without a care in the world and I was sorry that I was the cause of her muted celebrations. I never felt this predicament was my fault of course because I'd had no choice in the matter, but I was just sorry she'd had to go through this.

"Hello Sam, Big Mac, Help"

By New Year's Eve I'd had quite a few goes of the speaking valve. After a few efforts I started to make noises, much to the excitement of Sam and Politeness. But I just sounded like Chewbacca from Star Wars. I was quite encouraged but was still wondering exactly 'how' I would talk. Would my throat feel different like my right ankle had, then I'd start talking? Was it to be a slow formation of sounds becoming clearer and clearer?

That morning about 9:30am Politeness turned up at my bay. She had a steely look of determination in her eyes I'd not seen before. "Today you're going to choose two short phrases to say through the speaking valve. Think about how you would greet Sam and choose a type of food you want to eat if you become able to." 'Yes ma'am' I thought. She was still polite but very definite.

HELLO SAM I communicated for my first choice because I needed something short and unemotional. If I managed it I didn't want to cry a lot as had been happening since the strokes. Then there was the food item to choose: BIG MAC Ooh, I could've murdered one. It was two months since any food or drink had passed my lips.

Politeness got me to try and mouth the words. My lips weren't moving much but I gave it a go out of the left corner of my mouth. Sounds came out again but nothing intelligible. "Try again but take a deep breath first then speak through the breath this time." 'Okay' I thought 'My breath isn't much, but I'll give it a go.'

"Hello Sam" I said. Politeness raised her eyebrows "You did it!" Keeping calm, I followed up with "Big Mac." Feeling confident, I made a bit more effort with the soundings, over-emphasizing the words like I used to in my youthful drama days. "That's even clearer" Politeness said. 'Sam will be here soon' I thought, 'Keep practising.' "Hello Sam, Big Mac" I went on.

Then Sam arrived. She was looking straight at my eyes as usual expecting me to dart them around communicating that I wanted the alphabet board. Politeness remained silent as she knew what was about to happen. "Hello Sam" I said. "Oh, my goodness!" she exclaimed, clasping her mouth. She was totally floored. "What do you want to eat David?" asked Politeness. "Big Mac" I said. Sam welled up and Politeness shed a tear as well because she could see what it meant to us.

How did Sam feel? For those of you who've had children, cast your mind back to when they first said your name – then multiply that by one hundred. That's how she felt. It was sheer exhilaration. For me, I could be understood even though my voice sounded slow and computerized, quite nasal like a station announcer. I was pretty sure that was the effect of the trachea. We kept the speaking valve in for a few hours that day and more words just tumbled out. But after a few hours I was exhausted, so Politeness removed the valve till the New Year break was over.

One morning just after the New Year I had a bad incident. I had indicated to the nurse what position I'd like to be moved electronically to in the bed for the day. After a few minutes I realised I'd got it badly wrong. My head was tipping too far backwards to rest on the pillows. To avoid my natural gaze being towards the ceiling panels I just held my neck forward a bit. It was an effort holding my neck up making the usual excited wait for Sam very exciting. Very soon my neck became like an uncontrolled wobbly head making it painful and awkward to breathe.

I glanced at every nurse going past, but my face was still expressionless making them oblivious to my pain. Sam wouldn't arrive for at least two hours, so someone had to help me. At first I was angry: 'Who wants to stare at the ceiling all day? Don't the nurses think I look odd? Would they be comfortable sitting like this?' My neck gave up within thirty minutes so I couldn't even turn my head left or right. Breathing was now getting beyond difficult. I could see a nurse out of the corner of my right eye. "Help!" I screamed. Surprisingly sound came out even without my speaking valve in. But it was very quiet like I was far away. "Help!" I tried harder but couldn't get a deep breath.

My initial anger had long gone leaving only helplessness. Once more I tried "Help!" The nurse turned her head. "David, was that you?" I was too weak to nod so I let the tears streaming down my face do the talking. "You don't look right. Let me get you some pillows." She lifted my head up and squeezed in two more pillows. I did an automatic deep breath now my windpipe was clear and the deep pain in my neck subsided, and relief filled my heart. 'Thank you, God.' I thought.

Getting Ready for Putney

IM GOING TO WORK SO HARD AT PUTNEY "I'm sure you will, Dave. If anyone can, you can" said Stuart. Tour Guide at Putney had told Stuart those who respond best to rehab were those with an athlete's mindset. Stuart knew I had one of those because he'd seen me grow up with the desire and determination to win at most sports. I was blessed with the inner hatred of losing. But he also knew that after twenty-six years of marriage, ministry, and kids, I wasn't exactly demonstrating it much. I just watched sport on TV now with milk and chocolate in hand. I had been blessed with good hand/eye coordination, had loved the challenge of sport and they were a winning combination for me. But too much of a good thing can be a bad thing and so it had proved to be for me. In my adult life I suffered from the 'been there, done that' attitude to sport and its challenges had been replaced by those of property development and building churches. The middle-aged spread had well and truly set in, and I was lethargic to all sports now.

This time though I had not been there, and I had not done that (i.e. recovered from four strokes, total paralysis, and locked-in syndrome). The renewed motivation was refreshing. I had a completely new challenge ahead of me and one I had to win. The added dimension this time was there was no opposition and no trophy because I was competing against myself.

By this time, a healthy fear had begun to grow in me of not wanting to be disabled for the rest of my life. It came with an appreciation for life and limb that I'd not known before. This devastating brain stem stroke had awakened the athlete's mind in me and the hatred of losing to my middle-aged, lethargic self would also drive me on. I felt like I was back to my youthful athletic days on the long jump runway of life, and all my family and friends were gathered round to see if I'd jump the qualifying distance – normality. The normality of all of our lives had been affected by these strokes and my aim was to get back to as near to that as possible.

For the last couple of weeks at Lewisham and for the first month at Putney I was in this weird 'in between' phase where other people were in control of my voice. If I had my speaking valve in I wasn't locked-in and didn't need the alphabet board but when my speaking valve was taken away I was locked-in again and needed the alphabet board. Every day when it was time to take my speaking valve out it felt like the nurses were taking my voice away, the perils of which were perfectly illustrated by a visiting specialist nurse who noticed my cuff was down. She just put it up again without asking. I was fuming. The air disappeared from the back of my airways, and I was back to breathing solely through the trachea. I didn't have my speaking valve in so I couldn't tell her – I was locked-in again.

Fortunately, when she invited Sam back into my bay she noticed by the indicator on my trachea what the nurse had done. "Oh, what have you done? Why is David's cuff up again?" Sam questioned indignantly. The nurse said it must have been a mistake for someone to have left it down, so Sam immediately put her straight on my recovery and the nurse profusely apologised and put my cuff back down. Ah, air in my nose again.

All across Christmas my right bicep had been getting a little of its strength back and I became able to lift my forearm up a couple of inches off the mattress. The Sisters took great joy in shaking my extremely weak right hand every morning when they saw me trying it. But try as I might I could not lift the elbow. It felt like someone had welded it to the bed. I couldn't even lift it a millimetre to make the mattress expand under it. "They'll do something about your elbow" the nurse said, remarking about Putney. "They have their ways. Not everyone would do it their way, but they get the results. A friend I knew who worked there said she saw miracles every week." 'Hmm, miracles' I thought 'I think I'm having one of those.' She'd forgotten she was talking to a minister.

The day before I left Computer Man noticed my oxygen saturation was a little bit low. It was annoying because I had come off all oxygen a few weeks back and he wasn't giving the observations machine the usual time to settle before taking the correct reading. I didn't have my voice in so I couldn't tell him to wait a bit for the reading to go up as it normally did. 'They'll do something about that at Putney' I thought, not letting the situation annoy me.

On the penultimate day, Politeness came to say goodbye. "I'm not in tomorrow for your last day so I thought I'd come and say 'Goodbye'." She'd done a smashing job on me. A job - how satisfying. Her job was my life. Not really a job but more of a vocation or a calling like I had. "I've had to change your report for Putney three times over Christmas because your speaking and swallowing has made so much progress." I couldn't say 'Goodbye,' so I just smiled back with the left corner of my mouth and nodded my head appreciatively with a little queen's wave of my right hand. Even if I could hug her and say "Thank you" it wouldn't be enough. I had so many people at Lewisham to thank - what in the world could stop me from coming back one day to thank her and the ward nurses?

One of the specialist trachea nurses came past that day as well to say her goodbyes. When recounting the unlikely progress I had made and she felt I would make at Putney, she jokingly exclaimed, "You should write a book!" – little did she know.

The Last Morning

Bruiser had been running our room for my last night and she knew her care of me was over. As she walked away from my bay that morning she slowed, turned round, raised her chin and looked down her nose at me. She held her arms high and mimicked washing her hands of me. She must have held on to the upset of our complaint against her all that time. How disappointing, I still shake my head in disbelief that someone in the caring profession could do that.

Tranquillity came out to see me and say her 'goodbyes.' She'd been very calm and professional throughout but this time she let her guard down. I could tell this was a person to person 'goodbye' not a therapist to patient one. "I hope it goes really well for you at Putney. You've made great progress." There was compassion in her voice for my predicament. My speaking valve was packed so I couldn't say goodbye to her. I really wanted to and I think she knew it. She held my right hand in both of hers and gave it a tight squeeze. "God bless."

Sam arrived early that day just after 9am. She was going to follow in the car behind the ambulance. The transport drivers arrived with a thin, hard, trolley and high bars to stop me rolling off it. This time when I was slid off my bed onto the trolley's surface, I could feel it. Last time I was slid from surface to surface for my night-time intensive care MRI scan I couldn't feel it. So much had changed and was still changing; I was off life support, I could speak, I was starting to swallow and had some limb movement.

As I was pushed out of my room my right-hand moved too slowly to give a wave that would be noticed by Mr Belvedere, and my two other roommates opposite were otherwise engaged. Dribbly Starer was nodding to communicate 'Yes' as a relative helped him spell out a word using a copy of our alphabet board. They had seen Sam and I chatting away with it these last two months and wanted that same level of communication for their family. Politeness had taught them how to use it and I was very happy about that. We'd been able to help someone even when being locked-in. Burping Escapee was half-hanging out of his bed as usual. He did actually escape from the ward once, developing diabetes rapidly unbeknownst to the nurses and had a fit. He was rushed to intensive care, but he survived and was returned to us. It seemed a bit of a desperate way to escape and I'm glad he failed.

Being wheeled down the corridor I could see into the other rooms as their doors were wide open. Screaming Lady stopped as I rolled by, distracted by the activity. She was sat up on her bed with her legs crossed and had a harrowing look on her face, a look I'll never forget. I wished I could have said 'goodbye' to the nurses as I was wheeled out of the ward. They were so good to me here. 'What would the nurses be like at Putney?' I thought.

'Ah, outside air.' I could breathe it in through my nose now. I was 'cuff down' and could feel the cold January air filling my nasal passages and throat. In my last transfer I was 'cuff up' and didn't have that simple pleasure – how I'd missed it.

It was a rough transfer, and I felt every speed bump and pothole this time. The trolley felt as hard as nails as I had gotten used to the soft hospital bed for the last two months. I was lying flat, and my back was really aching like it did every morning when the nurses flattened my bed to change me. But this ride took over an hour and my back was killing me. I could see traffic lights, flats, skylines, and clouds which were beautiful to my eyes despite the pain. I was appreciative of so much now – I was alive.

Eight
I'm Disabled

Looking down over my chest and feet I could see the open ambulance doors. Beyond the hive of nurses, the ambulance transfer drivers, and my oxygen tank I could see The Royal Hospital for Neuro-disability, Putney, with its imposing Victorian architecture and manicured gardens. Others decided I should come here, others brought me here, and I was welcomed by others. I was getting used to trusting others with my life. I felt overwhelmed again by it all like I had felt in intensive care, but I knew it was for my good and just went with it – not that I had much of a choice.

My New Home

Being wheeled along its grand, cavernous corridors to my new room the transfer drivers and the staff enjoyed some banter. It set me at ease because I was becoming apprehensive in my new environment. My last hospital arrival had been unconscious, but now I was totally with it. What if my oxygen tank tubes catch on a doorknob? Do these staff know I'm not locked-in? When can I have a suction? I desperately wanted to talk and explain my situation and feel a bit of control, but instead things were just happening to me.

I was spun round into my room from the newly refurbished ward and brought to a halt next to my bed. After the ambulance drivers slid me on to it, a nurse said with an authoritative voice "We'll take it from here." Relieved that my aching back had eased, I sank into my new spacious bed. It was so big that no more 'repositioning' in the night hours would be needed. It had been a constant battle to resist the gradual slide down the bed at Lewisham even though I was lying like a racing driver.

With my property developer's hat on I could guess my private room was about three metres square. There was space for my trachea station, cupboards, and a disabled sink. The door slid into the wall, obviously for wheelchair users. In front of me on the wall was a TV – nice. How and when I was going to watch it though was anyone's guess. It was unnervingly different to Lewisham but at the same time intriguingly different.

The lady who had 'taken it from here' introduced herself as the assistant matron. She was a loud, stocky, Portuguese women. She introduced herself and explained "This is your call bell. Press this whenever you need something, like a suction, and someone will come." She used her finger to indicate pressing the orange disk shaped button on the white computer like mouse then put it just behind my hand. She told me she would be overseeing a lot of my care, especially my trachea removal process.

Overseer smiled a nice full smile and walked out, but just as she was leaving looked back and started sliding the door shut. "How do you want it? Like this?" (half closed). I was horrified being only used to an open ward. I shook my head. I needed a suction, and they might forget about me leaving me to drown in my own saliva. She had not put my voice back in so I was locked-in and couldn't speak. She was shutting the door now and could obviously not hear my gargling breathing. I no longer had Mr Belvedere to speak on my behalf. "Like this?" She pulled it closed so I could barely see her eye. I shook my head furiously. "Like this?" Finally, and to my great relief, she opened it wide. I nodded vigorously knowing that would give me the best chance of having my breathing heard. "Oh, okay." Overseer looked bemused, shrugged her shoulders, and walked off. She didn't understand what it was like to slowly drown in your own saliva.

'Right, I've got to try and press this call bell fast. I'm running out of time before I drown.' My elbow was welded to the bed as usual, so I had to try and stretch my hand under itself and reach it. I managed to get some purchase on it but try as I might I could not grip it because my wrist and fingers just weren't strong enough. Before I could start panicking Sam's smiley face appeared. In all the commotion and the distractions of arrival I'd forgotten she'd been following behind. "Hello darling. Oh, you need a suction. I'll sort it out." 'Why had Overseer not heard my breathing if Sam could?' I thought.

Night and Day

Sam found out all the new procedures to acclimatise herself with Putney and found out that I needed clothes enough for a whole week. We only had enough for a day or so thinking they might be put on me every so often for an occupational therapy exercise or something. But they were going to dress me and put me in a wheelchair every day – so different to Lewisham but splendidly normal.

I didn't like the first night at all. When I saw Sam the next day and she arranged, much to Overseer's consternation, for my speaking valve to be put in I sobbed "Take me back to Lewisham!" The trouble was I couldn't reach or press the call bell despite it being just behind my palm. That night was spent in memorable helplessness as the night nurse walked on by and I had to wait for my gargling breath to get so loud they'd hear. I experienced that horrible drowning sensation far too much that first night. Not sleeping much had its own knock-on effects of tiredness mixed with stroke fatigue (which came in unannounced waves) making it difficult for me to concentrate and retain loads of new information and names.

The following morning was a real mix of encouragement, discovering the disabled life, and learning about my new physicality. Out of nowhere a girl appeared in the corridor outside my door about 8:00am, peering into the staffroom and watching day nurses have their 'handover' meeting with the night staff. A patient obviously, she must only have been a teenager and she was already dressed and walking around. She looked like she was going to fall over at any moment because her legs and frame didn't look strong enough to hold her upright. Wobblys' face was expressionless and her voice monotone. She didn't look right but a thought occurred to me, 'They've probably got her to walk here.' Seeing her walking greatly encouraged me.

The staff meeting finished after forty-five minutes, and a little queue formed outside my room as a few staff members took turns to enter and wish me well during my stay and tell me that they were a Christian too and were praying for me. I was not lacking prayers here either. Patients started to appear, either wheeling themselves in wheelchairs or being wheeled by a member of staff. One older man was going so slow he took about thirty seconds to get past my door, but he was only giving the wheel rims the tiniest of pushes for some reason. It wasn't at all awkward. A black male carer walked slowly past, carefully carrying trays of breakfast, saying his good mornings to passing staff in an American accent. I hoped the trays of food would be for me soon. I couldn't imagine what eating again would be like. Until such time I was still on burger sauce at night times.

After my fourteen medications had been squeezed into my stomach tube by a nurse (here nurses only did medical work and made the medical decisions) a lady appeared with smooth dark skin and tight dyed blonde afro hair. "Good morning, David. Welcome to the RHN, Putney!" she said with a smiley face and commanding voice. She was a health care assistant and was obviously in charge of caring for me that day. In Charge wore dark blue trousers, a purple pin-striped blouse, and black shoes.

All the staff had to learn about my specific disabilities. Was I fully cognitive? What was my temperament? What parts of my body could I move that they wouldn't have to? The carers never knew what they were going to be faced with from a new patient. I guess that was their standard 'first day' approach: a loud booming voice with a wide-eyed smiley face as if talking to a baby. When they got to know me with my voice in there was a notable change of expression and tone, 'Just a taste of the misunderstood disabled life to come' I thought.

I still didn't feel the need to have a cover sheet at night as my inability to regulate my internal body temperature meant I didn't feel the cold, so just a towel it was. Air temperatures of hospitals are always too hot, and I didn't want anything on top of me anyway because experiencing paralysis with sheets on compounded the feeling of being buried alive as I was too weak to move them.

Dressing me and changing the sheets was horrifying. In Charge and her colleague dangled me over the side of the bed without the bed bars up causing my heart to leap into my mouth. If I hit the floor it was going to be face first as I couldn't react with my arms, and that was going to hurt. In Charge had me on my side holding my hip whilst her colleague washed my back and legs. To them I was safe, but I was petrified. Dressing me in clothes was something they obviously had down to a T given their speed and nimbleness with my limbs. They even gave me a choice of clothing. I nodded at one top but didn't really care 'I'm not here for a fashion parade' I thought, but I appreciated the empowerment behind asking.

Next, into my own wheelchair via a wall-mounted hoist. It was huge like the Lewisham one with head pads. They tilted it backwards and squeezed me into it. I couldn't self-correct if uncomfortable, so the carers were careful I was comfortable. They did all this with a tube hanging out of my stomach, a catheter, and a trachea. 'Amazing' didn't cut it.

Then something odd happened. I was unable to control my left leg. It naturally wanted to lock at the knee and sprang awkwardly forward. When the carers put it in place on my footplate it started to vibrate violently. 'So this is how it's going to be for now' I thought, feeling perplexed. Being so paralysed I felt vulnerable and out of control and such random limb movements were disconcerting. The right-side limbs which I could move slightly were floppy at rest, jerky when tensed. I was cumbersome with no coordination. For someone who had good manual dexterity from sports this was unnerving. It could have been embarrassing but the carers had obviously seen it all before and didn't bat an eyelid. My left leg eventually calmed down of its own accord.

I'd hardly had chance to start processing this all before I was spun round to the sink. 'Now your personal care' they directed. That was brushing my teeth, hair and them offering me a shave, but that would become my dad's preserve and a son's joy. Having someone else brush my teeth first seemed like a form of torture and certainly not a glamorous job for the staff either. Because I was nil-by-mouth, after brushing they had to use dry wipes to soak the water out of my mouth because I'd lost the ability to spit and they had to push their fingers between my teeth. Imagine that - carers wondering if they'd still have a full set of digits at the end of a shift.

Sam fixed the call bell situation first thing that morning by arranging for a big red button on a bendy blue stem to be positioned just above the back of my right hand which was a welcome relief to know I was safe again. The whole experience of that morning was night and day from before the strokes – I was an adult in what seemed a baby's body and had to be treated as such. I felt dehumanised.

I Was Fortunate

Sam would soon be waiting outside my door every morning but getting used to a long, two-hour rush hour journey across London was going to take time, so she wasn't there yet. The staff wheeled me down the corridor into the Day Room filled with other patients and left me to wait for her.

For me at that time in my recovery it was a sombre experience. I would not go back to spend any real time there until my last day, and if I did, it would be for a specific purpose. I wanted to be surrounded by family and therapists because I needed encouragement and inspiration towards the normal lives they were living. But in the Day Room I found myself surrounded by disability and it made me think of what I was, not what I wanted to become. I knew I couldn't afford to visualise disability if I was to keep my recovery going. This wasn't denial but just the mindset of a competitor.

There was a young man to my left with wispy legs sat in a wheelchair like mine, unable to lift his neck so his expressionless face stared continually at the floor. There was an old man chewing his cooked breakfast unnervingly slowly with his eyes shut. Behind me was another older man wheeling himself around shouting uncontrolled racist expletives and to my right was Wobbly, sitting in a regular chair staring expressionless at the TV. Next to her and talking at her as if there was an engaging conversation between them (there wasn't) was a slightly older girl with a trachea like mine, complaining in child-like fashion about her sporadic dizziness.

I wanted to be moved to where I could see Sam coming down the corridor towards Drapers Ward. But I couldn't grasp my wheel rims let alone pull them. My voice was in, but still with shallow breath my calls for help were no match against the humdrum of room noise. I felt trapped in my body for the first time since the strokes hit.

I was understandably upset by this but was shocked to find that I started shaking with frustration, my limbs spontaneously stretching, and I found myself panting for breath. A nearby staff member thought I was having a fit and moved me to address the situation. It wasn't a fit though, just an extreme emotional response to the feeling of being trapped in my own body. I needed time to get my head round what just happened and time to calm down before Sam arrived.

I found this all very off-putting and I didn't feel like I belonged even though I looked and moved similarly awkwardly to everyone else. I'd been the 'someone' who was 'always worse than you' in St George's, but now I wasn't. I still had all my cognitive functions whereas some patients here had sadly lost some of theirs. Yes it was a negative experience, but it also had a profound effect on me for good; I know having the strokes was a devastating curve ball but I was so fortunate in comparison.

Discovering Disability

Thankfully, Overseer took me off the oxygen tank soon because she understood about temperamental observation machines, unlike Computer Man back at Lewisham – that was another tube gone. Just as well because I found out I was going to have a shower twice a week and didn't like the vulnerability of having an oxygen tank hanging around. How were they going to shower me? In a full-body hard plastic tray on wheels with a flannel protecting my trachea, that's how. I felt vulnerable even with that anyway, but it was worth it to feel water running all over me again.

It's one thing for me to trust a trained professional to shower me with a trachea in, quite another to trust a gleeful Samuel pushing me at speed down a corridor towards a 'relaxing' coffee shop. To be fair I did ask him to (which I think he enjoyed too much) because I thought the rush of air through my hair would be a great reminder of running (not that I had much hair). Samuel needed to get comfortable with my profound disability and this was just a small thing he could do to help in that process. Being 'parked' out the way by the family while they queued for their coffee was an understandable necessary evil I had to learn to accept at first, but we eventually all agreed I should be included with them in the queue going forward.

The whole family had to get used to me living in a wheelchair: learning to frequently adjust my seating position to un-ache my backside, adjusting it smoothly without me being flung forward, learning to walk as a group slowly together without the others leaving me and the person pushing me behind without realising it, or not forgetting my 'trachea emergency kit' which had to be kept on the wheelchair at all times in case of drowning – you know, little things like that.

I DON'T WANT UNIVERSITY TO SUFFER ANYMORE is what I started saying to Sophie. I was okay with her coming to see me on Saturdays only now, not midweek as well as she had been in Lewisham, and she needed permission from me to get on with her life without guilt. Life was going on and my recovery so far was heartening for her, so I wanted to set her at ease to enjoy university life and focus on her course. For Samuel though it would be a few months till he went back to school full-time. There's never a good time for strokes of any kind but this was especially bad timing for him because he was starting his GCSEs and was obviously finding it hard to concentrate on schoolwork whilst processing everything.

One of the good things that can be revealed by disability is just how sensitive, kind, and compassionate families can be. We saw Sam's sister more than ever before, not least because she lived twenty minutes away in Surrey, but also because her 'big sister' mindset kicked in to look after us more than ever. Running errands, co-ordinating practicalities, looking after their Dad more to free up Sam – it was wonderful because I'd never had a 'Big Sis' before, as she affectionately became known. My family, usually so competitive and direct, showed their caring side by being very warm and affectionate. Both my brothers and Dad kissed me on the lips every time they visited rather than just Mum, which filled me up emotionally. Mum and Dad took to tucking me up in bed again every night they visited like when I was a kid, checking my bed position, pillow placement around my body, and stretching out my left-hand fingers.

The therapists were doing their own tests of me to guide where to pitch my rehab, and so I took this on board and did a little test myself one Saturday morning. A volunteer approached my bay offering to take me to play a communal game called Petanque. When she explained what it was I thought I could use it to see just how strong my right arm was. It was recovering a bit, so I wanted to see what it was capable of.

Two lines of about eight patients, each from other wards or institutionalised patients, faced off against each other in a grand hall. The aim was to throw your small, weighted ball as close as possible to the white jack in the middle of the hall between us. The only thing was none of us could throw. Some had their arms and wrists twisted in unnatural, unusable positions, some were paralysed, and others had arm movements but no control. To accommodate this the volunteers had a long yellow chute which, if we couldn't release the ball, they placed just above your chest so you could aim and release the ball from under your chin into it. For those who couldn't control their necks that much the volunteer would do it for you after taking your nods for aiming left or right.

I wanted to try and see if I could throw the ball and not use the chute. Part of me didn't want to use the chute because I didn't want to have to accept I was that disabled, the other part of me just wanted to see what I could do with my slightly moving right arm, so I knew what I had to work with. Even though I was left-handed that arm was still paralysed so I had to try with my right. I couldn't do over-arm so under-arm it was. I just about managed to hold the ball and throw it before it slipped out of my grip. It just dropped directly onto the floor and didn't even go beyond my wheelchair. The volunteers held up the yellow chute to my chest and I had to release the ball from under my chin. It was both humiliating and a reality check. I might be dressed in a wheelchair and with all my cognitive functions, but I was like a sack of potatoes in it.

On Sunday mornings there was a church service patients could go to, and as a minister I felt obliged to go along that first Sunday. The same grand hall used for petanque was now packed with wheelchairs and people with all sorts of disabilities - I lost count there were so many. For the first time in many years I wasn't leading the service. I was free just to enjoy it, but at the same time I had space to think about what had happened to me. Tears streamed down my cheeks and my face screwed up when the chaplain introduced a song I'd loved from my childhood. I could no longer sing, but my heart could, and sing it did. The purest worship I'd ever known ascended secretly and silently. I was so thankful I'd survived.

I was brought back down to earth by the chaplain when I realised he was singing the song solo. 'Of course,' I realized 'no-one else can sing either.' Strangely though it wasn't a great experience overall. I had been wheeled in late and parked side-on at the front where I could see everyone. Looking at the many and varied conditions that people had it pulled my spirits down like it had in the Day Room before. The desire to be surrounded by normality welled up in me again because I didn't want to be disabled and needed all the encouragement I could get at the start of rehab, so there and then I decided never to go back.

I felt awkward for a few Sundays when I'd have to explain to willing volunteers who came to collect me that a church minister didn't want to go to church. It was strange for me to feel that way about things too because I would have been a volunteer helper at that kind of service before I got ordained and always felt I was helping people. I explained my conflicted feelings to the chaplain who'd led the service when he did his weekly rounds to willing patients. He was very gracious and perfectly understood my need for encouragement.

Offended

When things inevitably got on top of Sam and I in the early days we just talked it out or communicated about it (depending on whether my voice was in or not), being great sounding boards for each other. We'd always try to end on a positive note by listing my progress: 'Don't get excited but… I can touch my nose, my knee bends, my ankle's fine,' and so on.

The main reason things got on top of me was I was interacting now so much with the normal world. Hoisting, showers, wheelchair rides, therapy sessions, I was always being made to do things I couldn't do. Most people don't spend time thinking about these things happening to them, I know I certainly hadn't. It was thrust on me overnight with no symptoms of gradual decline over years. 'Don't have a stroke' was my advice to others in those early days (when my voice was in). 'Of course not!' the carers would joke back. But my mind would also dwell on that Sunday service experience and the feeling of survival I'd had, pure thankfulness like I'd never known. It was going to take time to digest these feelings and adapt to the present realities.

I was not in a stroke ward now but a hospital for neuro-disability. No one here said, 'You've had a stroke' or 'You've suffered from locked-in syndrome' rather they talked about your 'brain injury.' It was a phrase I found strange at first, but it was a medical term I found helped me deal with the massive thought that I was now disabled. It enabled me to logically entertain the possibility of getting better because I now understood neuroplasticity. I was starting to realise there was going to be a long, tiresome, in-between stage before being okay.

Most of the time I never really felt my disabilities were going to be permanent because of my divine ICU experience. But in the meantime I felt I was going to have to handle peoples' misunderstandings about my condition, possible prejudice, maybe humiliation and condescension. But I decided I would never take offense because if I was learning about my new condition other people most certainly would be – I would need a lot of grace for people. There was opportunity everywhere to be offended, take language for example: Was I going to be 'a person with disabilities' or just 'disabled?' Were other people to be 'able-bodied' or 'physically normal?' Make no mistake, these can be important to people because the terms affect self-esteem, mentality and perceptions. But I just plumped for 'disabled' and 'normal' for simplicity's sake.

There were a lot of things I didn't like about being disabled: the loss of choice, the loss of a healthy sense of independence, not being able to do anything about the dry skin amassing on my lap from my face, being low down all the time, my body having a mind of its own. I looked disabled, sounded disabled (like Darth Vader with a cold), and my body moved disabled. There was no getting away from it: I was disabled.

Nine

Boot Camp

In my second week at Putney it was my forty-seventh birthday. Not how I thought I was going to spend it, but we made the most of it, nonetheless. We booked a family room to have a private celebration. There was a feeling of optimism in the air because after the first few days adjustments it was obvious to us all that this was the best place for my recovery.

A kind car-loving carer rushed out to get me a present. He kept raving about his BMW with a soft top all the time, clearly very proud of it. Beamer got me some T-shirts and a cake for everyone else to enjoy. Though I couldn't eat any of the cake nor blow its candles out it felt so good to do something normal.

In the middle of the party I suddenly remembered something exciting that had happened the night before. Sam has recorded in her diary what happened next. *'At the party, David was keen to tell me his right arm had touched his face last night. As he was telling me this he unknowingly lifted his elbow up from the wheelchair armrest to show me his hand touching his face. This was the best birthday present ever because he'd been waiting ages for his elbow to lift!'*

Trachea Out

Shortly after my birthday Overseer started me on the process to get my trachea removed. Not only did she have a thick accent, but she also had hearing aids, which is probably why she had not heard my need for a suction the first day. We laughed together that with my shallow breath, quiet voice and only the left corner of my mouth working, our communication might not be the best – but we didn't do too badly.

I had to repeat a similar 'cuff down' process to the one Politeness led me through in Lewisham. But this time it was for learning to tolerate the speaking valve. "They have their ways," was what a nurse from Lewisham had told me about Putney. They were right because I could already tolerate it for most of the day but she started me back from only two hours the first day (which is probably why Sam had to fight for my speaking valve to be put in for the first few days there). I went smoothly through the two-week process till I had completed forty-eight-hours with 'my voice' in. It was extremely tiring and many times I fell asleep or gave up speaking due to running out of puff, but Sam and the family understood and just kept cheering me on regardless.

That part of the process was going well but I was still needing suctions at night. This started to concern me. How could I exist without a trachea if I still needed suctions at night? The answer was I couldn't. Fortunately, the night nurse happened to speak with me about it. He was Ghanaian and had an extremely deep baritone voice. 'Dave, if you're going to get off this trachea you need to relearn how to cough and manage your own saliva,' said Baritone one night. Light bulb moment. That's it – I had to dislodge the saliva from my airways myself. I had a go, but it was a pathetic result. I couldn't draw much breath and I certainly couldn't hack out a cough. But over the next week Baritone and I worked together on my coughing technique (I didn't know there was one) and reduced the number of suctions needed per night from five down to one.

The day arrived to have my trachea out. I was so keen for it that I asked one of the staff members to get me out of bed before their usual 7:45am 'handover' meeting, and without a wash. I sat there in my wheelchair by the light of the moon excitedly waiting for the moment when breathing air through plastic would become a thing of the past. After the handover meeting I was told that there was one last hurdle to go and for that I'd have to wait till 11am. This was to wear a red cap totally blocking my speaking valve airway for two hours so I would be forced to breathe normally. When it was put on though, it literally felt like someone was strangling me because the plastic attached to the trachea still dangled down my throat. I even had to do a physio session with it on where I remember thinking 'Forget the session and just concentrate on breathing to stay alive.' It was nothing like normal breathing and to this day I don't know why consultants still enforce this last step.

When the two-hour mark was reached I expected someone to appear and remove it, but they didn't. Within half an hour I was starting to feel faint, and Sam noticed my speech was slurring. She walked speedily across the corridor into the staff office to ask for help. The staff member quickly found out that it was the physio who'd just taken my session who was responsible for signing off on my trachea process and said she was in a meeting and wouldn't be free for a couple of hours.

By now I had my eyes shut with my head slumped to the side. My oxygen was low, and I was looking pale. I just wanted to sleep. When I heard the member of staff report back I summoned up every ounce of strength and started shouting, "Get this trachea out now! Take it out now! I'm dying here!" I didn't stop shouting. My whole body was shaking with anger and started to spasm in all different directions. They had no idea what I was going through.

As if by magic, the male lead physio, Tour Guide, entered the room in a rush and took command of the situation. "Okay David, calm down. I'm going to take your trachea out now." I was desperate, "You better!" I retorted, still shaking and squealing. "Is it out yet? Is it out yet?" I yelled frenetically. I felt a hand pressing a bandage against my throat where the trachea should be. "It's out" came the reply as Tour Guide sealed the small hole.

I sobbed and sobbed deeply with relief; the air felt so wonderful in my mouth. I was filled with sheer exhilaration and the realisation that my breathing had been released after two-and-a-half months. Sam also shed tears of relief as she clasped my right hand. We both couldn't speak for crying. I knew she understood how I felt, and I knew the future for her had just got a bit brighter. The overriding thought I had going through my mind was 'Something's normal again.' I no longer needed assistance to breathe: no pipe, no medication, no green emergency pack everywhere I went, no more suctions with bodily writhing, no drowning sensations, no burning left thigh – just pure easy breathing. This seemed like the first major step towards recovery had been completed. Don't get excited but... I could breathe through my nose and mouth permanently.

According to Overseer, I'd completed her trachea removal process the quickest she's ever known and without any setbacks. "You're fast becoming our new poster boy!" she exclaimed. In truth it was down to the work of Politeness at Lewisham, and Baritone. I told Sam how thankful I was for his advice and a few days later when he covered someone's day shift I was able to introduce Sam to Baritone. It was a case of hugs all round.

I could say normal things now whenever I pleased; I'd joke with the carers who brushed my teeth in the morning "Promise I won't bite" when they stuck their finger in my mouth to dry it; I could ask them "Can you put the bed bars up when you change me;" I said to Dom my brother-in-law "Thank you for shaving me back in Lewisham." It also meant no more alphabet board. I will never again take talking for granted.

A Naked, Murderous Vicar in the Shower with a Young Girl

The first two weeks at Putney were for basic assessments of my capabilities so the therapists could work out what in my body needed their focus in the timetable they were developing for me. Three incidents in those first two weeks really impacted me: a shower, a tilting table, and some psychology.

Occupational therapy is primarily concerned with being able to complete day-to-day tasks around the house and my arms and hands needed to work for me to be able to complete these everyday tasks. My right arm and hand was freer now it had been unwelded at the elbow since my birthday and my occupational therapist needed to figure out what tasks I could and couldn't do with it. She was a young, slim, Irish girl, and had clearly mastered her profession having worked in different settings. I was confident in her ability to help me and over time we forged a good relationship.

Task Master hoisted me naked into a special shower chair with wheels that was brought to my bedside. It was tilted back, so there was no risk of me falling out. I was surrounded with large towels and then pushed to the large wet room. It's the first time I'd ever been naked with a young woman other than my wife. It was especially weird for me being a church minister as well but just part of the job for her.

I couldn't grab the shower head next to my right shoulder, so Task Master placed it in my right hand. Though my right arm progress had been exciting at Lewisham, this shower and the petanque throwing experience were a reality check. All I could do was slightly aim the shower head towards my left leg until my right arm collapsed onto my lap. Nothing else on my body moved significantly when sat in that position.

When I saw my left leg I was stunned. It looked withered and spindly like a starving child's from Africa in a charity fundraising leaflet. Where had my long jump calf muscle gone? Where were my cycling thighs from my sporty youth? Can nearly three months of total paralysis cause this much muscle wastage? How am I going to get that back if I can't even stand? There was a bit of shape to the quad muscles around the knee which would explain how I managed to push away Tranquillity at Lewisham in her physio session, but the whole left leg also awkwardly stuck straight out by itself. By contrast, my right leg was reduced in size a bit but was even all over and sat properly on the shower chair footrest. I didn't like what I saw and found it very unnerving because it was a severe reality check.

The second experience was rather more encouraging. I gave Tour Guide a similar stumbling experience to Tranquillity from Lewisham with the strength of my quads. Physios were interested in the legs and feet and by some bizarre logic also breathing (hence Tour Guide's involvement with my trachea removal). As a result he scrapped his planned session and said, "Let's go straight to the tilt table!" He hoisted me up from the blue padded plinth he had laid me on and swung me over to the tilt table. He wanted to see how vertical he could get me on it whilst strapped to it. I'd felt I could stand on my legs since Lewisham, and this was now the safe way to try it.

As he slowly started to raise me to a near vertical position, I took in my encouraging surroundings. In the centre of the brand-new gym was a lad hobbling around playing basketball and shooting hoops, in one corner there was an older man walking with the aid of a hoist on a treadmill, and there were people scattered round the edges sitting at tables doing tasks with their hands. Everyone was disabled to some extent and restricted in movement, but everyone was moving. It was just what I needed to see after the shower experience, very inspiring.

I started to feel my weight gradually increase through my feet. What a wonderful feeling it was. Instead of it being an emotional moment I just thought, 'How do I get from here to walking?' Emotions got the better of Sam though who was faithfully watching on. I knew she wanted to stand with me but that would need to be for another time because there was too much activity going on around me. I was almost vertical and talking when just a couple of months ago I was horizontal, paralysed and blinking.

Third, and most unexpectedly, was the psychological testing to which I was subjected. Thinker had introduced himself to me that first day when I was blotto. I just remember thinking, "I won't be seeing you again, I'm all there." How wrong I was. Thinker scheduled three sessions of two hours each with me.

It was explained that because I'd survived the rare 'locked-in syndrome,' he wanted to check if I was fully cognitive. Sam was politely uninvited to these sessions so I would not be influenced or distracted by her in anyway.

Much like Sophie's 11+ practice papers, the tests were extensive and tricky. Grammar tests, word meaning tests, memory recall tests, shape pattern tests, the lot. I hadn't concentrated that much since my Oxford ordination training. I did incredibly well to concentrate since I had yet-to-be diagnosed sight and hearing issues, strange sensations all over my body, and my reading glasses broke halfway through the first session.

Reading from a script that he told me he could only say once, we got going. "These tests are designed to make you fail. That way I can find your level of cognition. So don't worry." When I understood that I just relaxed into it. After three sessions of two gruelling hours we got to his last test. "This last test is the hardest.

I'm going to show you fifty images, then afterwards ask you out of a choice of two which one I showed you." I didn't have the best memory, so the only way I was going to have any chance at this was to try something outrageously funny to lodge the images in my mind: I imagined how each object might murder someone. A Christian minister ought not to think like this - but it worked. I got forty-nine out of 50. Thinker and I were both stunned, and he asked me how I managed to get such a high score. You should have seen his face when I explained.

Thinker arranged one final summary meeting that Sam could attend. "David, your results place you in the top fifteen percent of the whole country." Before I had chance to express my surprise, Sam burst into tears. They were tears of relief. She'd been unsure of my cognition ever since the strokes because of early mistakes I'd made with the alphabet board, and now my trachea was out but I still sounded disabled she was confused. I said to them both that though I looked funny and sounded funny I was "the living embodiment of not judging a book by its cover." Thinker gave us the report of the tests to give to the DVLA, "You'll find it easier to renew your driving license with this." Right now driving was a stratospheric impossibility but his comment got lodged in my brain.

It Was in the Atmosphere

The result of these and other therapy tests was that I was placed on their most intensive of rehabilitation programmes. It was like a school timetable. It was so full of sessions that once I even had to ask Task Master to schedule in rest times because I fell asleep in one of her sessions. One Friday afternoon my body just gave up and shut down - a weird experience if ever there was one. Managing the fatigue and staying on top of the tiredness became of paramount importance if I were to survive such an intense programme. Early on I couldn't stay awake much beyond 6pm after days that full.

The schedule for the following week would be put up in my room on Friday afternoons meaning I had all weekend to admire the torture planned for me. IM GOING TO WORK SO HARD AT PUTNEY is what I had communicated to Stuart back in Lewisham and never a truer word had been blinked. It felt like a military boot camp, but I loved it.

It was an intensive programme because my many tiny improvements were so rapid it was wise to strike while the iron was hot. I was not in control of some of these improvements – my brain was just making new neural pathways and some of the strength I originally had was still there. Throughout my right side particularly, I was discovering that strength was evenly distributed among the muscles and tendons, and nothing was twisted or out of place. It was all incredibly weak like I'd never known weakness. I could hold someone's hand but couldn't hold onto it if they slightly pulled it away. My hand's movement was becoming less jolty too. The right shoulder strength was slightly returning, and my neck was no longer noticeably wobbly. Apart from a little bit of strength in the quads my entire left side just limply lay there. My back and core muscles were lifeless too.

But what I was starting to come to cherish was the all-pervading atmosphere of Putney. 'You're here to get better' the staff and therapists would often say. It was so encouraging, and you really believed it. It was officially called a hospital, but it was known as a rehabilitation facility. The health care assistants, consultants, doctors, and nurses existed to let the therapists do their job, and there was a great harmony between them all to this end.

As well as my individual programme, there were general sessions open to all patients to deal with the common issues associated with brain injuries. At the only session I went to, there was an older lady with her husband in attendance and bizarrely they both had the same name. But it was because she mouthed words to her lip-reading husband that they caught my attention. She had a trachea and couldn't speak, similar to how I had been, but because her face wasn't paralysed she didn't need an alphabet board. It struck me then the many and varied ways a stroke can manifest – they just destroy parts of the brain randomly. I could see those sessions would be helpful for some who were faced with learning to live with their disabilities, but I wasn't at that stage yet and didn't really want to know about my brain injury. I just felt to focus on working hard to get better and knew I could ask the therapists at the appropriate time why things were happening to me.

Twenty-Five Minutes

Julian trekked across London to see me again, but there was no blinking about MOURINHO now. He was just thrilled with the contrast to his previous visit: No alphabet board but talking and sitting up, dressed, in a wheelchair and not lying down totally paralysed. It was a wonderful time of laughter, normality, and prayer. Clive and his wife Jane were equally amazed when they popped up. Though I was still nil-by-mouth, on a catheter, and in a huge wheelchair, they were having a conversation with me. When I slowed because I was running out of puff he just laughed saying, "Anything's better than that alphabet board." He wasn't wrong.

We'd also invited Mick and Wendy again so we could give them some sad news. I'd been told in intensive care to "Leave Belvedere." It was now obvious why: not just to do more writing but because my recovery was going to take a long time. Sam had been right all along because we weren't in Belvedere for a long time after all. I wasn't looking forward to telling him our news, in fact Sam and I felt a bit awkward arranging a relocation back to Surrey without them knowing first. But they were wise enough to know after their first visit in Lewisham that despite my surprising survival, I would have to leave. We told them our plans and unsurprisingly, they had already resigned themselves to the fact we'd be leaving but not without first giving us some words of encouragement. "This will turn out to be a doorway into something new." The sense of purpose I'd been feeling throughout all this grew some more that day.

The inevitable finally happened and I was asked to move rooms now the trachea was gone. Though I'd been in a ward of four men before in Lewisham, this felt like a watershed moment in my recovery. My new bed was next to a window looking out over the car park exit to the A3 beyond. It led straight to Surrey which made me think about our new home, the completion of which had just taken place days earlier. When Sam moved into it from the church house in Belvedere, her journey dropped from over two hours one way to just twenty-five minutes. It was a huge relief to her that the buying process was over because so many things could have gone wrong, but mercifully they hadn't. In fact the estate agent said it was the quickest purchase he'd ever known.

She felt immediately at home. With both of our families around her she was back where we'd both grown up. Free of the location constraints of ministry for the first time in our married lives, Surrey was at last our home again. No longer were we priced out of its housing market either because of our families financially coming together to help us. I owe a huge debt of gratitude to them for that.

Jealousy

For the first time in my life, I experienced jealousy when I least expected it. It was mixed with empathy though when I got to know the three other men in my new room. Opposite me was an extremely obese, multi-million-pound construction business owner. Middle-aged, married and with kids, Big Money was still part of the weekly clubbing scene. By his own admission, his stroke was brought on by his boozy, calorie-laden lifestyle. He had no feeling at all down his entire left shrivelled side ten months post stroke. He had a sunken head where part of his skull had been removed and had been stitched into his side for safe keeping. That procedure released pressure in his brain and saved his life, he was doing rehab whilst waiting for it to be put back.

I wished I had Big Moneys' normal voice, mouth, and eyesight but I felt very sorry for him that he had an unresponsive left side and his skull had been cut away, whereas my left arm and leg were responding in miniscule ways by now and my blood clot had dissipated naturally in ICU. His timetable was busy but not as intense as mine – he didn't have any sessions before getting out of bed like I did sometimes.

Diagonally across from me was the young Irish lad I'd seen on my first morning in the Day Room. He was the thin, withered, expressionless lad who couldn't hold up his head. He shook his entire body to communicate 'Yes' (you can get so much more attention with that than just BLINK). But he was able to write though with a hand placed on a writing board, and according to his mum could still write complicated mathematical equations. I felt so sorry for him because he'd just finished studying computing at university and was on a lads night out celebrating with his mates when he had his brain injury. On his way home in a drunken state, The Math Lad made a split-second decision to cross the tracks between platforms at a station and got hit by a train. He had his whole life ahead of him but now this - so sad. The Math Lad had quite a sparse timetable but understandably much of it was spent with Thinker. I could only imagine how he was handling the regret; I wasn't jealous of him.

On my right was a slim, single older man. He was the guy who had trundled slowly past my door on the first morning in his self-propelled wheelchair. He had a stroke when he was driving his bus. A passenger managed to call an ambulance and saved his life. Bus Driver could talk, albeit slowly but with clarity, as well as wheel himself around. He could also brush his own teeth, reach for his own deodorant in a high cupboard, and make phone calls.

I was jealous of his manoeuvrability, dexterity, and pronunciation but then again he slept a lot, and I mean a lot. Once he slept for two days straight. The carers and therapists did all they could but try as they might, he wouldn't budge. I had suffered fatigue initially but was now managing it well with pre-emptive lunch time rests but his was something else. It was so bad he hardly ever used the toilet but just relied on his nappy and let his carers discover the fact. And when he was awake he watched a lot of TV with hardly any visitors. His timetable looked alright to me - a good balance I thought - but he missed a lot of sessions through sleeping. I was glad I didn't have that level of fatigue.

The last thing any of us was contemplating was driving, but since Thinker had mentioned it Sam kindly wheeled me outside for the first time to see our car. Since my strokes it was the first thing I had asked to do to help remind me of normal life going on outside. I wanted to see and touch our new car that we'd just bought before my strokes with an inheritance. It was a bright, windy afternoon and my eyes took a bit of time getting used to the sunlight. Sam pushed me right up to the dark, sleek SUV we'd named 'Black Shadow' for a joke. It was huge next to me in my wheelchair. As I felt the driver's leather seat, I thought to myself "Will I ever get back in this car, let alone drive it?" It seemed such a long way off being able to do what Thinker alluded to. I couldn't even wheel myself in my wheelchair or hold myself properly when sitting up. Beamer saw my whole experience through a window and on my return said, "Mr David, you have a Range Rover – I want one!" He was joking, I think. How could he be jealous of my car when he had his soft-top BMW?

"I'm Baaack!"

It was Valentine's Day and Mum had hatched a plan to buy Sam a card and chocolates from me, and I had tried to write a simple 'I love you' message in the card. The pen was placed in my right hand, and I managed to write lightly in the card in childlike fashion before the pen fell out of my hand. It was a real accomplishment especially as I'm left-handed.

Sam came in dressed up looking especially gorgeous, gave me a kiss and sat down. She looked more restful after her new twenty-minute journey on the A3. "I've got you a card and present in the cupboard behind me" I told her. She was beside herself, and when she opened the card she was reduced to tears. This scene was unimaginable last November. On one level it was a meagre gift compared with how I felt towards her for her devotion, for her belief in me, and for her capacity to handle things at home. On another level we both knew it represented such advancement, and after all it's the thought that counts.

That afternoon when my sessions had finished we played our favourite board game together whilst listening to our favourite radio station in the background. We always used to do this of an evening. Sam was better than me at most games it seemed, but for some reason I excelled at this one. Without glasses, and with my as-yet undiagnosed stroke related vision issues, and with cards balancing on my knee which Sam turned over for me I still won. "I'm baaack!" I squealed in a high-pitched voice as I unsuccessfully tried to hold back the accompanying excessive laughter. We both thought it was hilarious and started to reminisce – it was such a lovely moment.

Contrasting that, I saw something around that time that will stay long in my memory. The lady who had the same name as her husband was moved out of our ward upstairs to long-term residential care. It's a polite way of saying that you need more care than four daily home visits from carers can safely provide. It means you're going to be institutionalised for the rest of your life – exactly what an intensive care consultant predicted for me. It was a sombre moment and a reminder of how close I'd come to that fate. She had a trachea like I had but wasn't able to progress on the 'cuff down' process. She'd been on a bus ride with her husband and carers to see what life could be like living with a trachea, but it was too much for her and her husband to live like that. They'd obviously come to a very difficult decision about her future. I watched as she was wheeled out of the ward and the doors closed behind her. And there was me wondering about driving 'Black Shadow' again.

But we were all on our own journey and I had to keep recovering…

David preaching at Belvedere Baptist church

Ten

Fight Back to Normal

It was the depth of night, and all was quiet, but I was awake and still in my private room at this time. I was thinking about my divine survival against the odds and all the work therapists were doing with me. A thought kept going round and in my mind: 'If mercy has got me this far then I've got to do something as well.' God does what He does i.e. my survival and neuroplasticity, and I do what I can do – which was going to be exercising. My recovery was to be a partnership. I wasn't to 'down tools' and wait for something to happen, rather it was already happening, and I was to show respect to divine mercy and not take it for granted. It was a light bulb moment – I already knew this in my head but now it was in my heart and my quality of life was going to depend on it. My youthful vigour was awakened from its middle-aged slumber in that moment.

It wasn't difficult to find any motivation. Firstly, the thought of being disabled for the rest of my life was haunting me. It wasn't the thought of disability itself that didn't sit right with me, it was the thought of not trying to do anything about it. If I could do something about it then I should. I couldn't live with disability if I'd not tried to do something about it.

Secondly, it was so encouraging to think that only three months ago I was in intensive care, totally paralyzed, on life-support, with a trachea, suffering locked-in syndrome. Now I was alive, no trachea, talking, and experiencing some movement in my right-sided limbs. The thought of experiencing a full life at home after surviving and recovering from something like this was tantalising.

Thirdly, I felt there was a purpose behind my present circumstances. I had already realised just before my strokes that my future lay in writing and speaking about mercy. Now I was motivated to get better so I could do just that, and what an experience of mercy I was having.

Fourthly, there was my family. I didn't want their lives to be blighted because of my suffering. Sam had so much life ahead of her, Sophie needed a father to walk her down the aisle, Samuel needed a father for guidance, and I should be looking after my parents in their later years – not the other way round.

I just wanted to be normal again in short, but I knew it was going to be a fight. I'd never felt at any stage up till now that I was consciously 'fighting for my life,' but now I did because I realised I could do something about it.

A Shock

I thought the first thing I would need to be able to do was to be able to get out of this bed myself. I didn't want to be bedridden for the rest of my life waiting for others to hoist me out of bed every day. For that to happen I would at least need normal stomach muscles again and in my mind that meant only one thing – sit-ups.

I was shocked when I tried. I managed one. And by one I mean I could only lift my neck up. My torso didn't even bend, and my back stayed welded to the bed. There and then I paused and thought, 'What am I getting into?' I thought of every muscle group in my body and what it would take for me to develop them to be able to sit up and then walk around. I thought about the number of hours I'd need to exercise for and for how many years that might go on for. It would take ages. I gave no thought to life after Putney, what that might look like or where it might be if I couldn't walk. I just felt I had no choice but to start if I wanted to be at all normal again. So that became my rehab aim: a fight back to normal.

I had done a few years of weight training as a teenager, so I knew exactly what I was getting into – the endless repetitions, the minute gains over time, the sweat and exhaustion, the pain. I didn't want to go through all that again for good body shape, I'd been there and done that. But this time I needed to go through that again for normality. Three sets of ten 'neck ups' were dutifully completed. I was exhausted and fell back to sleep.

I didn't do any daytime exercises at first because of regular family visits and scheduled sessions. But the tone was set. The next night I was awake around 3am and having fallen asleep around 7pm I'd already had eight hours. I used to wake in the early hours for listening prayer, so I was used to being awake at this time anyway.

This time I thought about my left arm. It was in bad shape, especially my hand. That was put in a furry brace all night to keep my hand from being a claw. But I'd wake up in the morning to find it had worked its way free of the straps. Every yawn or spasm would cause it to spontaneously close, so I thought I'd leave that for a therapist to look at first.

My arm was a dead weight, so I had to try and do something with it. I tried with all my might to lift it off the pillows that it rested on. There was no movement, but I could feel the top of the forearm slightly tingle, so that was enough to go on. Three sets of ten tensing the forearm followed. Forget the dumbbells of my youth, now my arm would be the dumbbell. Three sets of ten reps for my neck followed then I succumbed to tiredness. This went on for a few more weeks.

My Life's a Gym

When I got in my new room and became much more aware of how other patients were further forward in their recovery than me, I found I was getting even more motivated by competition. Big

Money could already sit up by himself with one hand. My nightly 'neck ups' would need to progress along with right arm strength for that.

One night I heard Jolly Dancer talking to Bus Driver and it piqued my interest. Jolly Dancer was a hilarious Indian night carer who would dance and sing overtly between patients as he did his duties. When I told him that Stuart happened to be a Hollywood script writer/director he crowned himself a Bollywood wannabe to his own fanfare and started waggling his neck with palms raised upwards as he danced around the ward!

He asked Bus Driver to shuffle back on his bed after he'd been put into bed so as to get comfortable. I needed to be able to do that too. I would at least have to be able to do some kind of movement lifting my core using my neck and heels as anchors. So to help I invented a new exercise: ladies and gentlemen I give you 'The Reverse Plank' – not that I could even do one yet. I was just so inordinately weak and felt so heavy. But I could feel the strain throughout my body like I had in my left forearm, so that was enough to encourage me to keep going. This and other miniscule exercises I thought would help me added about half-an-hour to my burgeoning nightly routine. It was tiring like you would not believe (some nights I remember exercising with my eyes closed) but wriggling gave me a bit of freedom, and after suffering internal and external paralysis it felt glorious to be able to move ever so slightly.

Within a few months the exercises started to pay off in helpful ways. I could just lift my neck and shoulders off the mattress, and I was able to do a slight bridge when the carers dressed me in the morning – no more being balanced precariously on the edge of my bed whilst being dressed. They had a time limit to get every patient ready in the mornings so any help I could offer was gladly received. We're only talking small things don't forget, like lifting my right arm a few inches to help it being fed through the sleeve or lifting my neck to go through my collar more easily. At least once-a-week though it would be Beamer or another physical carer's turn to get you out of bed. It was his job to make such basic tasks an exercise no matter how long it took. My heart leaped when he showed up in the morning because it meant a few minutes longer of vital exercise – my life was becoming a gym.

One evening as I was being put to bed I had a thought, 'I wonder if I can do away with the cast on my left hand?' I would need to be able to lift my left hand up from my side to my tummy and correct any clawing of it into a fist with my right hand. This would test whether the monotonous tensing of my left forearm had amounted to anything. I didn't ask the night shift carer to put on my hand cast that night so I could attempt the lift.

With the carers gone and the lights off, I started the test. I began inching my forearm further and further up my ruffled towel that covered my mid-riff, having rests every so often to prevent exhaustion. A few times I slumped over my right arm and tried to grab it with my fingers, but it was either too far to reach it or it would slip from my grasp – so close. Quite frankly I was too excited to give up and finally I did it a few minutes later. I stretched my left-hand fingers and rested them on my tummy under the weight of my right hand. Exhausted, I fell to sleep relieved. When I woke up later that night I thought 'I wonder what new exercises my arm can do from this position?' I was just relentless like this and couldn't stop trying new exercises because the tantalising possibility of normality was worth the effort.

My daily routine kept getting better in those early months at Putney with massive gains… like being able to press the 'On' button of my electric toothbrush with my right thumb. The encouragement I got from Beamer and Task Master one morning made me feel like I'd just climbed Everest, but these were life changing things for a once paralysed man. Of course straight away my mind turned to the call bell I hadn't been able to press on my first day. I managed to reach and press it instead of hitting my big red button a few days later. The light in the ceiling came on and sure enough a few minutes later In Charge appeared. "What can I do for you, David?" "Nothing thanks" I said, "I was just trying to press the button." It was a bit scary to rely on the call bell alone, but I had to trust myself and my growing abilities.

Shaving was next: My dad's gentle encouragement to gradually take over shaving was wonderful and encouraged by the therapists – I told Task Master to leave that one to my Dad and she, like the therapists at Lewisham, were wise to it. This goal would be a bit longer to achieve because I was realising just how many muscles were involved in a normal action I used to give no thought to. Fingers to grip the electric shaver, shoulder and bicep to get it to my chin, then the wrist to press it against my skin. I just managed a few dabs on the beard first time whilst straining and bending down for it, then my dad would have to take over as my arm would get tired quickly.

Keeping my left arm on my wheelchair arm was a faff. They gave me a special wide arm for it to rest on because it was awkwardly twisted and kept dangerously falling of the normal ones. After so much nightly tensing of my left arm I wondered if I could lift it back up onto the armrest instead of having to ask Sam or a carer.

One morning I had a go, just before Sam arrived at noon in case I couldn't pull it back up and she'd have to help me. It hurt, and felt so heavy, but leaning my whole body to the right I managed to do it after my first aborted attempt. A few minutes later I recognized the 'clonk clonk' of Sam's heels down the corridor. She walked in the room, her usual bubbly self, and straight after we kissed I said, "Don't get excited but... look what I can do." To her horror, I pushed my arm off the armrest, so it dangled limply. To her joy and relief I pulled it up first time, just skimming the edge of the armrest. Task Master arranged for a normal armrest after I showed her.

Crash

I learnt the hard way that weekends were for rest and recharging and not exercising, because early on I'd start losing focus by the following Thursday and feel mentally exhausted and fatigued. I really came to appreciate the difficulties of those with chronic fatigue syndromes. They have to learn to pace themselves while battling other people's expectations of them, like my cousin Richard's wife and daughter. You're going to crash later in the week if you don't rest, even when you appear fresh.

So one of the things I did for a complete change was get wheeled down to the Day Room to practise typing on the patient computer. In Charge was usually roaming around and was the only carer who knew how to play with the equipment and settings to make it work. She knew so much about every little thing I was convinced she'd be a matron at some point in her career. I'd have my back turned to everyone else so their conditions wouldn't affect me mentally. I was a two-handed touch typist before my strokes at about sixty words per minute thanks to Sam's tutelage. Now I'd be lucky to type six words per minute. I'd get physically exhausted after each line and my right arm needed regular rests. Having spent forty-five minutes trying it the first time I sat back to admire my efforts... I'd done a few short paragraphs.

Weakness is a strange thing. When I'd reach to press a key my right hand would shake over the keys under the strain and my shoulder would feel like it had iron wrapped round it. I invariably hit the wrong key and would have to reach for the 'delete' button and try again. By which time my forearm felt too heavy and my whole hand would collapse on the keyboard causing the cursor to type something like 'gyjde87j'. I would have to rest about thirty-seconds then try again. It was soul-destroying at first, but I came to accept it.

I was eventually given a special keyboard made from metal which instead of the having the keys sitting slightly proud, they were depressed. This meant I could let my hand collapse on the metal keyboard knowing the keys would be protected from my resting hand. Even with this I would need the keyboard pressed tight up against my stomach to be able to reach the top line of letters. Who'd have thought typing could be so exhausting? It would be another long goal like shaving.

Fire in Your Eyes

At weekends, the carers were more relaxed because there were no therapy sessions. I guess that's why we had showers then. One Saturday just after my trachea was taken out, the Black American male carer who carried the tray of food past my door that first day showered me. I couldn't talk very loud or clearly when lying down because my weak throat muscles and voice box would just collapse, so I tended to just listen and laugh a lot.

Like everyone else I had the pleasure of listening to his music and singing. He always played music loudly on his phone wherever he was. Everyone loved it and put in their requests. All the carers within earshot would sing and dance about as he belted out a wide variety of classic tunes. It made for a great party atmosphere.

Whilst showering me he paused and looked straight at me. "Dave, you're gonna be okay. You've got that fire in your eyes man, I can tell. Trust me, I should know." Then he shared something really private. "I don't tell many people this but…" He proceeded to tell me in great detail how and why he'd ended up in intensive care in his younger days. "I'm lucky to be here, Someone was lookin' out for me." Musical Gangster only just survived and months later he'd learnt to walk again. "I know what you're going through and what you're thinking… you're gonna make it." I should have been greatly encouraged but all I could think was 'How can he tell I'm determined just from my eyes?'

Musical Gangster went on to say something to me that even to this day I can't get out of my head. "I've seen patients here just give up because 'tings can be so tough." 'Give up?' I thought. 'How can anyone give up?' I couldn't give up even if I wanted to. I felt like I had no choice. I had forces beyond me dragging me towards recovery. Purpose, my competitive streak, my family, and the basic desire for quality of life. It may have looked like fire was in my eyes, but it was just pure logical sense. If I had reasons to get well (which I did), and I'd been given the ability to get well (which I had) why would I give up?

End of Days

The carers were extremely good facilitating us to get better. Their level of care was so good, but there were a handful that went above and beyond. Top-Notch Temp was a young Muslim girl well respected by everyone. She was only a temp but was requested to work by Overseer so often that we all thought she was employed there. I even saw some permanent staff ask her for advice in particular situations. She was so good to me that she even knew what time I preferred to go to bed, she remembered how I needed my room set up for night-time, and how to set it up in the morning – top-notch indeed.

I knew she'd appear at 6:15pm, ready to put me into bed. When I was put to bed I wanted to have tried so much with my rehab that day that I'd slump into bed exhausted. I knew I was onto something good at Putney, and I wanted to make the most of it. By 5:30pm I'd be clock-watching waiting for her to come. My right eye would be closing through tiredness and my backside would be sore from tolerating the wheelchair all day. By the time I got into the men's room the soreness had gone but my right eyelid was still closing. All day had been a fight back to normal and I needed those six to eight hours of sleep so I could go again in the early hours.

What Coming Out of Paralysis Feels Like

By this stage I was learning what it was like coming out of total paralysis. Generally, apart from the almost immediate lightness I had felt in my right foot, I was first getting the ability to twitch muscles internally whilst still feeling heavy. Either it began to happen spontaneously and in time became controllable, or it was controllable from the outset. I called it my reconnecting stage because I could feel and control muscle twitches in a certain limb but still couldn't move it. It meant neuroplasticity was occurring.

Once that happened it was only a matter of time before the twitching became visible and I could excitedly show an intently staring Sam. Depending on how much damage the strokes had done depended on where things went from there. Exercise would be needed for months until the limb became usable, then years to become normal. I was so encouraged by understanding this because my recovery now depended on me. Sometimes the limb might feel like pins and needles if the damage was slight or be twisted and feel like a sack of potatoes if worse, and in the extremities of my left side it felt like iron was wrapped round them. Stretching and working the joints was something Task

Master encouraged me to do a lot to help loosen my mummified state.

My Main Goal

When my night-time exercise progressed to actual visible movement the night staff would question me about seeing limbs move. Jolly Dancer would say "Mr David, why are you awake? Are you dancing like me? Are you okay?" "I'm going to be" I'd tell him. It was a bit embarrassing, but I just wanted to get well. "I'm exercising. I've already had eight hours sleep." The reason I wanted to exercise this much all the time was simple – I wanted to be strong enough to walk…

Eleven
Road to Walking

The moment arrived that I'd been waiting for - the time to ask the question uppermost in my mind. I'd been thinking about it since my right ankle started moving in Lewisham. Sam and I hoped we would get some specifics and not just "Everyone's different…"

"Will I Walk Again?"

After the first two week's assessments were completed, a date was set for our 'family meeting.' It's where all my therapists and consultants would share their results, answer mine and my family's questions and lay out their plan for my rehabilitation.

On the 28th of January we all piled into a tight, grey room for the meeting. After a general time of feedback each therapist was given a few minutes to lay out their assessment. I took it all in but was really only waiting for one assessment, even the initial discharge date of the 14th of April (which seemed alarmingly close) could not deflect my thoughts.

I was waiting for the turn of my new physiotherapist to give her report then I could ask her my burning question. She had not been involved with my initial assessment as she had only started in post the day before, so this was the first involvement we had together. I was glad to see her because I really wasn't getting on with my first physio which had been a source of great disappointment.

Through my speaking valve I asked my pointed question "Am I going to walk again?" On reflection - how was she to know? I put her in an impossible situation. I could tell by her face she knew the gravity of her answer could seriously sway my hopes.

"Everyone's different..." she started. I zoned out. What else could she say though? She only knew what she'd read about my assessments and what she saw in front of her – a mainly paralyzed, fat, balding man with a trachea (at this point) in a cumbersome wheelchair. She didn't know that I loved a challenge and am a driven person. She didn't know I was GOING TO WORK SO HARD AT PUTNEY and she certainly didn't know I was on a nightly fight back to normal.

What she'd read in her notes from my original physio was that after two weeks of daily sitting balance practise on the edge of a plinth I'd showed signs of self-correcting when my shoulder was prodded with a finger. Improvement from Tranquillity's sessions with me back in Lewisham, and with a full-length mirror. I looked a sorry state in those first two weeks. Staring back at me was an expressionless face, slumped frame with lifeless arms down by their sides and a weirdly twisted inwards left foot. But there was cause for hope; my right ankle was rotating as normal; I could hold my head up long enough to gaze at this person I didn't recognise, and I could see myself self-correcting which gave me one heck of an adrenaline rush. There I learnt what rehab was about: trying every day to do what you couldn't do.

I was a bit muted after my new physio's comments, and the whole meeting just left me wondering really. What would 'You're going to be okay' look like? Was I being unrealistic to think I'll walk again? Should I face up to a life of sudden, enforced disability? Might I walk a bit in years to come? I needed some clarification, some encouragement, and it arrived in spectacular fashion.

A few days later, through a series of circumstances beyond my control, I met a volunteer helper in a communal setting. She was a kind, older lady, wandering around chatting to patients. She introduced herself as an ex-patient which immediately got my attention. She had suffered Guillain-Barre Syndrome. It's an autoimmune disorder where the body attacks itself and can end in death or total paralysis – it's a rare condition, much like my surviving four simultaneous strokes and 'locked-in' syndrome.

She'd gone to bed one night two years ago perfectly healthy but woken up hardly able to move. She was single but had just managed to ring her daughter for help, who called 999. By nightfall she was in intensive care and paralysis had risen from her toes to her neck. What a terrifying ordeal to go through! Fortunately, the paralysis stopped there, and she survived.

She told me she had learned to swallow, eat, toilet herself, and walk again. Then she pulled out her phone and showed me a video of her taking her very first few steps unaided, explaining it had taken a lot of work to get there. I immediately asked her how she felt at the time. "Elated, and very tearful" she said without hesitation. When she was discharged she needed a bit of help from her daughter to get up and dressed but after six months she was fully independent. Now when she walked she said "...it's like pulling sandbags." You couldn't tell though because she looked normal to me.

I wondered if that encounter was a looking glass into my future. Was that what 'okay' could or would look like – pretty much normal on the outside, a few lasting effects on the inside, but going about your daily business as normal? I dwelt a lot on the reality of that. I was so encouraged I got her to meet Sam a while later. I knew Sam would be as encouraged as me and she was.

Cobbler

My first physio had misunderstood my attitude towards her physio sessions and had overseen my botched ending to the trachea removal process. I would tell her that I couldn't do certain things she was expecting of me – 'yet.' She took it as a negative mindset, but for me it was a statement of intent, meaning I was going to be able to do it someday.

You can imagine my delight when I was told of the staffing change and Cobbler came along. She used to work in a shoe shop in her youth and was an expert in sliding my shoes on smoothly. Her favourite phrase she'd say with a wry smile was "David, you know me, I'm just making it up as I go along." In my youthwork days it might have appeared to some that I was cobbling things together as I went along, but I always had a vast array of activities and presentations at my disposal through experience, so I understood what she meant. Experience with a bit of creativity, spontaneity, and humour goes a long way. We were going to get on great.

She took a lot from me; constant questioning about why my body was doing strange things; my sudden, embarrassing coughing fits in her face as I got used to managing my own saliva; even getting her to act out the things she was asking me to do (you forget a lot when you've been paralysed). She took it all in her stride and with great enthusiasm and sensitivity when it was called for.

By the end of the first week of February I was able to hold myself sitting up and self-correct where needed, so in a physio session with Tour Guide he left me and Sam sitting on the plinth alone in the gym whilst he ran to get something for the session. The plinth was just too high for my feet to touch the ground, so I felt precariously balanced. Two-and-a-half-minutes later he returned. After such a tragedy it should have been a lovely moment for both of us sitting side-by-side like the best friends we were. Instead I held my breath and was rigid, petrified of falling forwards. Ridiculous really, Sam would have easily corrected me if I'd started toppling forwards and Tour Guide would never have left us if I looked unsafe. But halfway through I managed to say to Sam with my eyes unromantically fixated on the floor, "Don't get excited but... we're sitting up together."

Standing Hoist

Cobbler had in mind all the possible 'roads to walking' there were. She needed to pivot creatively to make up a new road for walking for me that suited my body's recovery, so it was just as well she could make it up as she went along.

A good starting point was getting me out of using the overhead hoists and into what's called a 'standing hoist.' We knew there was strength in my legs, so this was a safe way of putting that to good use. It was safe because I had to be strapped into the standing hoist in a way that I couldn't fall if my legs collapsed.

I tried it that same first week with her. It felt so freeing to be standing on my own two feet without the straps of the tilt table. With my shoulders creaking with pain I leant on its forearm rests. My left claw hand was forced open and around the corresponding hand grip while helpers stood all around. "Lean forward" instructed Cobbler, as the machine whirred into action and pulled me up. "Stand tall" she said, interrupting my self-congratulatory thoughts. From then on we used the standing hoist all the time in the gym to transfer me from my wheelchair to the plinth and back again.

One morning a few weeks later I heard the familiar whirring sound of its mechanics in the bay opposite my bed. Big Moneys' carers had started using it to get him out of bed and immediately patient jealousy kicked in. "Why can't I use that?" I asked Cobbler at that morning's session. No 'Good Morning' or 'How are you today,' just a childish insistence. Fortunately, she interpreted my competitive edge as a positive. "We can work towards that" she retorted with her customary cheeky grin. She knew how to harness my motivation. A while later towards the end of February that same whirring was in my bed bay.

I would no longer be hoisted in or out of bed in a wall mounted sling. No more fairground rides as I used to call them, no more scary balance sensations making me feel like I might fall out. A carer came behind me to guard me should I need it whilst the other prised my left-hand onto the vertical hand grip before hoisting me into my wheelchair each morning. I was dropped once though because the carer didn't know my capabilities and didn't stand behind me. Shouting with fear I toppled over sideways from my sitting position but thankfully it was a soft landing on my bed.

That first day using the standing hoist in my bay was a great day because it felt like real progress. But at the same time I remember looking at its cumbersome size and thinking, 'I couldn't have this at home.' No sooner was I using it than I set my new goal to get out of it. So I thought about how I could use the standing hoist to get stronger ready for walking.

I'd realised the carers were getting me totally ready doing all my personal care before they changed my bed sheets each day. One morning I explained to Top-Notch Temp that I wanted to remain standing in the hoist for the five minutes it took them to change my sheets, then do my personal care afterwards. She knew how safe I'd be even if my legs got tired, so she cleared it with Overseer. I had nearly a month of standing five minutes per day. I could do all the exercises at night I wanted but there was no substitute for body weight through the legs.

Lightgate

Cobbler and I tried lots of different things to work out where my legs had problems and where they were working correctly, where they were weak and where they were strong. Primarily this meant having a good look and prod at my body. First Politeness from Lewisham fell in love with my Adam's apple, now Cobbler was getting up close and personal with my feet and legs. Under normal circumstances this would be 'unbecoming behaviour' for a vicar, but these were desperate times needing desperate measures.

Days after trying the standing hoist, Cobbler tried me on the Lightgate. It was an eight-foot-high frame on wheels that had a parachute hoist hanging from it. I was in that hoist dangling with my feet touching the ground and it didn't half hurt my crotch. I was warned by Cobbler that it might hurt and her male assistant that day just made 'helpful' wincing noises all boys make when a bloke gets a ball kicked in the goolies. His support was about as welcome as the 'support' offered by the parachute hoist on my family allowance.

Of Afro-Caribbean descent, he'd been working at Putney for forty years. He told me he'd seen some wonderful patient recoveries during that time which inspired me even more. He gave me hope that I might be one more of those wonderful recoveries. He walked with a limp, had a very 'happy-go-lucky' attitude and a wicked sense of humour. We bonded over our mutual love of football management computer games and weekly football scores. The Gaffer was a great physio assistant.

The Lightgate was both a disappointing and joyful experience. Disappointing in that there was so much wrong with me but joyful that there were some things right with me. There were also things Cobbler and I could do about some of the wrong things.

Hanging in the hoist I could see and feel my left toes pointing downwards and my foot inwards. I was unable to move my left ankle which just felt like jelly. Coupled with the fact that my left heel wouldn't drop down and touch the floor it made for a very disappointing walking experience. When trying to stride forwards on my left foot my weight would go dangerously through its two little toes only. This meant the ankle's weird position twisted out my hip which itself was extremely weak.

I asked Cobbler what I could do about it. "Activate your glutes" she said with a gleam in her eye. I didn't get why a smile was creeping across her face nor did I know exactly what my glute muscles were. "What are they?" I enquired. "These!" she laughed and squeezed my left buttock. I laughed excessively which was embarrassing but duly engaged the left glute and pushed my hip forward as instructed. She said it looked a better stance, but I felt like I was posing, shoving my left hip forward. It didn't feel right.

Then she turned me round so I faced the vast expanse of the gym. She wheeled the Lightgate forward and I was supposed to mimic walking. I could just do it with my right foot and leg, but when I pulled my left leg through it was rigidly straight like a plank of wood. This was not how I wanted my first experience of almost walking to feel like. I wouldn't have minded if both my legs were okay but just weak, but the left leg was also wrong.

She explained one of the issues for me was over-active quads. Both of us could do something about that. Cobbler introduced some sessions each week for The Gaffer and other assistants to run and I added more exercises to my nightly routine, pushing it well over the hour mark. Together we started to build strength in the left leg, hip, and glutes from an incredibly weak base position. My timetable and routine just got more intense, but I didn't mind because I just wanted to walk. It was the key to opening up my life again. I couldn't do much about the left foot and toes mind, neuroplasticity hadn't happened there yet.

Beat the Quads

One of the specific exercise sessions they tried to start me on was cycling on a special bike for wheelchair users. But my left hamstring was so weak, and my left quads were overactive that I could hardly put two rotations together before my plank of a left leg seized up and tried to spring forward like in my morning dressing times. The brain stem stroke and resulting paralysis had reduced the hamstring to a literal string, but this was where I could add another crucial nightly exercise to help.

If my left hamstring was drastically strengthened it would provide the biggest impact on my ability to walk, so I developed an exercise called 'beat the quads.' At nights I would try and bend the knee and bring the heel back to my glute. At first I couldn't do it at all, only feeling the hamstring tensing a little. But night after night I'd persistently tense it until I began to see movement. In all it took me a couple of months to bend the knee once and even then the quads immediately over-powered the hamstring, pinging the leg out again.

Naturally, the next goal was to be able to do it twice in a row and this took a similar amount of time – it was amazing just how weak the hamstring was. It could have been soul destroying, but I understood muscle growth and new eventually it would be okay no matter how long it took. I kept Cobbler up to date with what I was doing with my exercises like a chuffed little school kid to a teacher. To the physically able person it's hard to get genuinely excited about this, but to me it meant only one thing – I was getting nearer to walking.

Just after the clocks went forward and the evenings were getting longer I was doing 'beat the quads' at the end of the day. I tried the action for the umpteenth time without much success but suddenly felt my big toe move. I gasped and held my breath. 'Did that just happen?' I thought. Looking intently at my toe I did the tensing again and saw it move. I lay my head back on the pillow as tears welled up in my eyes. For the next fifteen minutes I sobbed the purest tears of joy, unnumbered prayers of thanks were offered for how mercy was unfolding, making me almost delirious. I knew I'd been saved from life in a wheelchair.

Because not all my left foot was working Cobbler tried to tackle another issue. It needed to regain some range in its ankle up/down movement so if I walked again my toes wouldn't drag on the floor tripping me up. This meant I had a lot of casts throughout my time at Putney in an effort to combat a calf muscle that had contracted like concrete forcing the foot into its pointing position.

Sam watched as Cobbler and Tour Guide wrestled this semi-paralyzed middle-aged man into position on the gym's plinth like rolling a walrus. I found the face down position necessary for the casting process stomach crushing, and because it prevented me from speaking Sam was on all fours relaying any messages I quietly squeezed out. It would have been a bad experience, but it was comical especially when Tour Guide was standing on the plinth holding my leg up whilst Cobbler slapped onto my calf and foot at speed dripping wet strips of quick-set wet plaster. Afterwards we all looked like we'd gone ten rounds in the ring with sweat and wet plaster spattered everywhere.

After weeks of effort Cobbler had done well to regain ten percent range of movement from my concrete calf back but we both knew it wouldn't be enough to stop me tripping. I had to accept I may have to walk with a limp for the rest of my life like The Gaffer because I wasn't sure what else could be done.

The Next Step Was Wheels

The next step in my road to walking was getting some independence by way of a less cumbersome, one-handed wheelchair. There's no two ways about it - I was slow at first. My right shoulder and triceps were painful with weakness, my grip was weak but didn't hurt much, and my ability to steer was embryonic to say the least. But I loved it. I knew it wasn't going to be a permanent fixture using one and it just fuelled my fires to get out of it eventually. There was no way I would be discharged on the 14th of April now as they had first suggested. I reasoned that if they were going to send me home, and I was WORKING SO HARD AT PUTNEY they'd have to send everyone home.

In one of my first independent outings around the corridors of the ward I embarrassingly came to a slow, grinding halt in the doorway of my old room, just like Bus Driver had on my first morning. Now I understood why he was so slow – weakness. I looked inside the room, but before I could reminisce about how far I'd progressed, there before me was the man who had taken my room. Previously a university professor he became known as the man for shouting 'Oh God, Oh God!' across the entire ward. He slept all day like Bus Driver, with both arms cramped up awkwardly on his chest.

He was on a FaceTime call with his wife when I awkwardly pulled up. His eyes were shut, and he could only moan and grunt in response to her questions. I saw myself and Sam as we'd been in those early days with me only able to blink to the alphabet board. I wondered what neuroplasticity he might get. I wondered how his wife felt seeing him like this. What thoughts was his wife having about any type of future? Waves of thankfulness swept over me as I gathered the strength to wheel away from this slightly embarrassing situation. I prayed for mercy for him.

Wheeling around the ward became a daily exercise for me. After a few weeks of doing so I started to wheel myself to and from some of my sessions. I was overtaken by walking staff members, caused traffic jams, held up people trying to use the lift, caught up by therapists who came to get me for my sessions, but I didn't care and nor did they. Every nurse, therapist and carer was just so happy to see me and others around me progress.

Cyra Steady

On the first day of using the mechanised standing hoist on the ward I devised a game called 'Beat the hoist.' I would try and stand up before the mechanism had finished lifting me. "Dave, what are you doing?" exclaimed Top-Notch Temp exuberantly. The hoist had gone slack, and I was standing up waiting for the hoist to catch up with me. "You don't need this!" she squealed.

Cobbler obviously got wind of this progress and started getting me to practise the next step of my road to walking in our sessions. It was using a new method of transfer that required more from my own body. It was called a Cyra Steady, and it had no mechanism or harness. It was basically a light blue chair on wheels and as I pulled myself up on the bar in front of me its blue paddles to sit back down on were shut. The paddles were slightly slanted, and it was an exercise just sitting in it for my core and quads. My right arm could help pull me up a bit, but my left hand still had to be prised apart, pulled forward and clamped on the horizontal bar. It was what my neighbour Mr Belvedere had been using back in Lewisham. I felt encouraged to be using the same method of transfer now that he had been using then. It was a great sign of progress. I wondered where he was – was he recovering like me?

After a few weeks of continued usage of the Cyra Steady in sessions, Cobbler was confident enough to leave me in it one time while she quickly ran to her cupboard to get something. She knew

I was safe under the ever-watchful eye of Sam, who was nearby as usual. Sensing an opportunity, Sam came over to me and stood directly in front of me.

I stood up to face her. There we both were face to face with only a transfer aid between us – the closest we'd been since the 2nd of November. There was no need for words or blinking as I started to vibrate and jerk awkwardly with tears running down my cheeks. She wiped her eyes while routing around in her pocket for tissues. We both managed to compose ourselves before Cobbler returned and she continued the session none the wiser. A moment of unspoken connection, relief and overwhelming joy had just unexpectedly graced our day.

The Cyra Steady was already being used in our ward by Big Money. He still had no feeling in his left side and was solely using his right side to lever himself up on it to get out of bed. I was a week behind him in using it on the ward but was using all four limbs. Bus Driver was ahead of us both using an even less supportive transfer aid. I was not ready for that yet and couldn't quite imagine being that sturdy.

Thankfully, Cobbler kept pushing me and by the 17th of March I was sturdy enough to stand unaided – the most notable day yet. Cobbler was one side, The Gaffer was the other, and plinths were in front and behind me. Maybe I wasn't sturdy enough to be jerked around on a more advanced transfer aid yet, but we proved together that I had it in me.

I lasted two seconds before I put my hands down in front and rested on the plinth behind me. "Hold on" I remember saying, "Let me try again" and I managed thirty seconds. Sam has written down what I later told her, "I could have done longer but it was boring." It was seriously encouraging, but we did uncover another problem. I felt decidedly unbalanced, and not just because of my left leg's problems or general weakness like Wobbly. I didn't feel steady in my head, like I was standing on a cross channel ferry, and it was most disconcerting. That would need looking into that's for sure.

Shortly after this, I completed my first 'Standing Group' session. Forty-five minutes of games and short exercises all whilst standing (with rest times too) in a group situation. I felt I'd been promoted. I was so excited to be progressing to this group with such speed. What in the world could stop me now from progressing to my goal of walking again?

Twelve
Why Not?

Months after I'd arrived at Putney, I found out that there was another reason I had been put on the intensive programme - because I kept saying "Why not?" to everything that was asked of me by the therapists. They told members of my family on more than one occasion that this positive, compliant attitude made me so easy to work with and would ensure I got the most out of rehab. I just wanted to get well.

No More Dribble

Occupational therapy, where I recovered enough of my strength early on to push my one-handed wheelchair, was a major chunk of my time in rehab. I was so keen for it that Task Master scheduled sessions for me every day for the whole time I was there. First we had to build strength back up in my right upper limb before I could attempt any daily tasks that I'd need at home. She set a daily forty-five-minute session of necessary, repetitious exercises to build my shoulder strength. I loved it, but because of my shoulder pain they needed to be extremely steady and controlled – no 'hoicking' allowed. I needn't do any nightly exercises for my right arm because of these sessions.

Sometimes we did the sessions at my bedside, sometimes we used the gym for a change of scenery. And we varied the activities that exercised the same muscles and tendons of the fingers, hand, wrist, arm, and shoulder – anything to break the monotony. From pouring water from a cup into another cup, to squeezing different thicknesses of putty with the fingers, we did it all.

I could mark my progress by how far I could reach up my face before my arm collapsed: chin, cheek, nose, eyebrow, hair, and eventually my crown. This was significant because after the first month Sam gave me a tissue to gingerly wipe my own dribble away. I had felt humiliated by the need for someone else to do that, let alone having the dribble itself – that must be how Dribbly Starer felt back in Lewisham.

One day, when Sam and I were reflecting on my right-side limb progress, I was complaining that my arm movements were not yet fluid. "My right arm still jolts around quite a bit" I said to her, illustrating the problem with my right arm. "What I want is to be able to move it more fluidly." When I said that I illustrated it again without even thinking about it. This time I did a perfectly smooth 'queen's wave.' We were both shocked and delighted at the same time. "Don't get excited but…" Sam laughed, as she rolled her head backwards and looked heavenwards with delight.

Ambidextrous Spiderman

I didn't know what weakness really felt like. I've felt weak and exhausted before, like after a long days' work on a property renovation, or once I could barely stand after I'd completed a half-marathon. I now realise that wasn't weakness at all, just tiredness. My right hand felt like it was restricted all over, like someone had wrapped a handful of elastic bands round it. I could just stretch out my hand as normal, but I couldn't hold it there before it collapsed back down under the pull of gravity. That's real weakness – when the force of gravity is stronger than your muscles.

I went back to the Saturday morning petanque game once more during this process just to see if I could throw the ball yet. In my first under-arm throw the ball went halfway across the hall this time. I was only there five minutes, and the volunteer chaperone

162

was most confused when I wanted to leave, but I'd got what I came for – progress confirmation.

When Task Master saw me hauling my left arm up onto its armrest I asked her if we could arrange an intensive plan for my left arm as well as my right. I remember her pause and her calculating look "Hmm, yes, we can do something. That's brilliant, David" in her Irish accent. 'Only a few months for it to catch up with my right arm' I remember thinking. How wrong I was. What I didn't understand at that time was the neuroplasticity had started later than the right side, which in turn meant more muscle wastage, putting it way behind my right. Task Master got her assistant to continue the right arm sessions and added to my already intensive programme daily left limb sessions. Although it was still clearly going to take one or two years of daily exercise to get it back to normal, the assistant confidently left me to it because I was doing the exercises myself each afternoon anyway.

Task Master got to work on my left limb. Each day she got me harnessed to a machine that supported my arm and shoulder muscles and put on me a black glove with black rubber bands mimicking my tendons to open my hand. It was a wonderful sensation to feel movement and openness in my limb again whilst doing all the activities she set me. I called it 'The Spiderman glove' though disappointingly it didn't sling webs.

One night a thought occurred to me: 'If I can hold the electronic bed control panel with my left hand and press its buttons with my right fingers I could control my seating posture.' To have that level of control back was too tantalizing not to try. As the carer asked me how I'd like to be positioned for sleep the following night, I held out my right hand as much as I was able and said, "Can I try it please?" She clipped the controller on my right-side bed bars and left me to it.

I managed to reach out my right arm, grasp it and bring it back to my waiting left claw-hand. Wedging it between its fingers my right-hand pressed the buttons. Though it wobbled a bit I was in control. Being a lefty, my right hand would usually assist my left in this kind of task but now circumstances were forcing me to become ambidextrous. It was unexplainably joyful to be able to use both hands together again, albeit in a painful and limited way, but these were the kinds of work arounds I'd have to put up with for the foreseeable future if life was going to work for me.

Music Rocks

I started using my left arm and hand at the upper limb music group instead of my right limb when Task Master started giving me left limb sessions. This group activity had been responsible for eventually producing my smooth, right hand 'Queen's wave,' but she knew my left upper limb needed more work than the right and this was a perfect opportunity. Three or four of us patients would be wheeled into a small music room that had loads of musical instruments that we could tap, strike, or shake along to music. It promoted rhythm, timing, and strength control. I'd totally lost my ability to tap in time, to clap, or click my fingers, which was unnerving at first for me as a guitarist. But, as with all things, persistence and repetition was the way to go.

I loved that group which helped make repetitious exercises fun. There were reps for the fingers, wrist, the grip, the shoulder, reps for everything the upper limbs might be used for. In our first session I was struck by how tight my right wrist was. It wouldn't move, so just to beat a drum along to the music I had to use my elbow instead of the wrist at first. But over time this loosened, and it became as normal again. Not so the left wrist. It was totally rigid, on the end of an arm that I couldn't lift, so the various instruments had to be positioned right up close under my dangling arm. In all my time there my wrist stayed the same without any rotation.

The funniest thing about the group was we got to choose the music. I always had plenty of song choices even though I didn't listen much to music. I expect they thought I was a right DJ, but the truth was I had spent the night before wracking my brains for songs of my youth or current songs I'd heard Sophie and Samuel listening to. Sam was more interested in the improvements my arm and hand were making though and would joke with me about her list of chores waiting for me at home. "You're the only man I know exercising so he's strong enough to do housework!"

Giggle

During my first two weeks I had been introduced to my speech and language therapist. She was of slim build, had mousey-brown long hair, and had a very smiley personality. Her sessions were nearly every day. She would always greet me quite distinctively at the start of our sessions by saying "Hello David" followed by a little giggle. I knew from day one we'd get on well and could tell she was as good at her profession as Politeness from Lewisham.

Giggle had her work cut out to improve my speech though. Let me explain. First, I had a locked jaw since the day of the strokes. Second, my lower right lip was totally dead. Third, this meant the lip rubbed on my teeth causing a large bump to appear. Fourth, my speech was slow (called dysarthria) like Bus Driver's with my tongue hardly moving. Fifth, the right-side of my face was stiff and not moving much and felt like a big bathroom towel was wrapped round my head – it left me looking expressionless when I talked. Sixth, I sounded like a station announcer as if I was talking by pinching my nose. Seventh, I was losing air out of my nose when I spoke because the muscle in the roof of my mouth, called the velum, wasn't working properly and let air out of the nose. When I tried to say more than three or four words I would need to take a breath. Eighth, taking a deep breath for a sentence was still virtually impossible because my torso muscles and diaphragm were so weak, feeling like iron bars wrapped around inside of me. How would I preach again with that much wrong?

Giggle set about getting her assistant to do daily mouth exercises with me. One of the exercises I really needed to do a lot was the one for my velum. It's a flat muscle in the roof of your mouth that when working normally would stop me sounding like a station announcer and stop my breath getting away from me. I needed this to work properly so I could preach in future. The embarrassing thing was the female assistant wanted me to make the 'ah' sound in quick, short, punchy sounds, acting as repetitions for it which makes for a very embarrassing sound.

In the wee small hours early on in Putney I was playing around with some of her mouth exercises. Suddenly the right side of my mouth noticeably opened a little. To me it felt like my mouth had been opened by someone – wonderful. In reality though it was only opened by a few millimetres, but it was the first time my right-side lips had been open enough for air to flow between them since the strokes. Sam noticed it immediately on her arrival. When Giggle arrived for her session she looked a bit startled when she noticed "David, has the right side of your mouth opened more?" "Yes, it started to open more last night" I replied. The door to preaching again just inched open a bit more.

A Big Mac Needs a Big Mouth

From drama without microphones in my youth to being notoriously loud at family gatherings and to preaching in front of large crowds as an adult I had developed an unfortunate reputation for having a big mouth. But just to be normal again I really needed one. So as far back as my initial assessment Giggle had started to work on my most pressing of needs: getting my jaw open so I at least had a chance of eating again.

She gave me extra-large lollipop sticks which nurse Sam was to wedge between my teeth longways and stretch my jaw muscles open. Over the first month each day we tried to increase the number she could squeeze in. For a baseline I could only do eleven whereas Sam could do twenty-three. We were told to do a few stretches of the jaw before we tried, to warm the jaw up, but progress was slow going. Sam recorded in her diary that we only got to fourteen after a month. It was a strange sight at the best of times with multiple lollipop sticks protruding from my mouth. But one day Sophie took the biscuit when she had a go helping me and right before she inserted the first stick she exclaimed "Wait. Which way does it go in – sideways?" Sam and I fell about laughing with images of Wallace and Gromit in our minds. I knew I needed a big mouth but that would have been pushing it.

To help speed things up one day I sent Sam to lunch while I had a rest and did continuous warm-up stretching for half-an-hour. On her return we managed eighteen. I did this each day for the next month before Giggle introduced me to the Therabite, a sprung-loaded hand device that would stretch my mouth safely beyond twenty lollipop sticks.

It was awkward and painful but worth it. Over the next month or so we used it repeatedly, leaving me breathing through a wide-open mouth like I'd just swum up for air from the devastating Tsunami wave that had overwhelmed me for four months by now. Ten minutes later my jaw would have retracted back but it was worth the pain for those glorious moments of relief. It became clear I was going to have to do these jaw-stretching exercises for the long haul to get it to remain open.

My goal of eating a Big Mac continued when Giggle took me for two 'camera up your nose and down your throat' tests. Since my first ever test with Surrey in Lewisham my swallow had got much better, but it was still too weak to eat and drink normally. So Giggle gave me ice chips to start with which was not exactly what I was hoping for after four months of nil-by-mouth. It was ice chips though because of the low chance of infection, but still, if it got me closer to my goal then why not?

It took me a good few weeks to be able to crush, suck, and swallow ten spoonful's of ice chips without coughing and choking. Giggle explained the next phase would be trials of thick 'n' creamy yoghurt, the prospect of which was truly mouth-watering. What in the world could possibly stop this next phase?

Finding My Second Voice

One day a middle-aged lady with blonde curly hair, casual clothes and a big smile appeared in front of me. Seated in my wheelchair she stood respectfully just outside my bed bay. She seemed to be fishing for business and her tone suggested she was used to rejection. "Would you like to do some music therapy as I play some tunes?" imitating playing a piano with her fingers. A grin broke out on the left side of my face "Why not!?" to which she seemed to raise her eyebrows in surprise. She didn't know my musical background but had struck gold in finding a willing patient.

Giggle worked closely with Tunes as time went on. They crossed over on pronunciation, breathing placement in sentences, volume control, note range – things like that. They measured the length of my exhale over time, they measured the loudness of my voice over time, they kept a record of the number of words I could speak before I needed a breath – all showed steady improvement throughout our sessions from a low starting base.

But the most notable experience was in the first session. My voice up till now sounded uncontrolled and badly out of tune and had dropped in range quite a bit. Tunes hit the middle 'C' on her keyboard suggesting "See if you can find that note." After a few seconds of warbling, middle 'C' could be heard to my great surprise. Not just because the note was vaguely controlled, but because I could feel it. It was indescribable exhilaration because I had found my lost second voice. I gasped, looked at Sam, and burst into tears. We had to stop the session there as I couldn't gain control of my emotions again.

Though walking was my main goal, singing again was up there with it because it was such a part of my life and faith. I hadn't realised how much I'd taken singing for granted. The voice box is a muscle and would take years to train again, like in the choir days of my youth, but I was more accepting now of the time my recovery might take.

After this and many other extremely emotional outbursts, sometimes angry ones too, I just had to find out what was wrong and what could be done about it. They were confusing and embarrassing for all who witnessed them. No-one was addressing them which we thought was odd because I was obviously not having normal reactions to situations. It was something I was becoming quite self-conscious about and being a confident public speaker that feeling was something I was not accustomed to. My emotions were totally out of control, and I couldn't get them under control. I needed to see the one therapist I never thought I'd need to see - Thinker. He knew exactly what it was immediately. "It's emotional lability" he replied. "Can I get rid of it?" I asked. "Everyone's different..." he started.

Not what I needed to hear but it was an interesting chat offering some hope. My brain had lost its ability to control its emotions because of stroke damage, so that ruled out a psychological problem. If neuroplasticity were to take effect in the corresponding area of the brain, control would be regained. Thinker said that if not I could learn to control it by thinking about an inanimate object that would distract me from whatever situation was causing the outburst whilst causing no emotional response of its own.

It was clear to me this would be a whole new way of life of actively detaching myself from the emotion of a joke say, a pastoral concern, or the emotion that music or a sporting achievement can create. I would be opening myself up to the misunderstanding of being emotionally detached from life but if I didn't, my perceived emotional reaction could cause great offense or seem inappropriate. I was going to be damned if I did, damned if I didn't. I would need time to take this in.

Let There Be Light

I had loads of appointments stacking up. I had a dentist's appointment to investigate my jaw and whilst under sedation they proved my jaw could open fully, so the Therabite usage would be worth it. An optician checked and found there was nothing wrong with my eyeballs meaning the visual impairment I was experiencing, like watching an old cine film with every fifth frame blacked out, was neurological so might improve.

It was early March 2020 when these appointments happened, and I was getting referrals to St George's for my eyes and ears (my balance issues could be linked to the ears but needed investigation) for May time. That would start the process of getting to the bottom of these symptoms, leaving me feeling positive about what the next few months would bring.

With the feedback from Thinker to hand, Giggle would often say, "You're operating at quite a high level." Meaning not that I was really clever, but that I was cognitively 'all there.' This was uncommon for the ward we were in because everyone there could communicate and express themselves in various ways but had lost some cognition. Some had enough cognition remaining to realise and adjust but sadly there were some who didn't realise they had lost some and faced a lifetime of vulnerability. I was incredibly thankful Thinker had diagnosed full cognition and thought I might need the documentation in future because currently I didn't look or sound it.

Because of my full cognition, in mid-March Giggle set me the goal of giving a staff presentation about my recovery. She did this to try and get me back into the groove of public speaking. I'd have a microphone to help with my quiet voice, leaving me free to focus on my clarity of speech and breath spacing; and the preparation of slides would be good exercise for fine motor movements for my right fingers (trying to use a mouse right-handed was proving a nightmare).

Giggle felt I had made suitable progress for this, and the assistant had moved on from mouth exercises to public speaking practice too. She printed out in large writing (we weren't sure what was going on with my vision) the first few verses of the Bible 'In the beginning, God...' and on through those classic words 'Let there be light...' We practised hard where to place the breaths to try and make the reading flow, which was tough considering I could only speak two or three words before needing to draw breath. It was painstaking at first, but slowly as Giggle and Tunes worked together I could get up to five words in one breath with intonation. I still needed to make up my own breathing points instead of using the punctuation of the text, but one thing was for sure – I wouldn't be preaching anytime soon.

Around that time one morning, the carers entered our room to get us ready for the day and whilst on the other side of the room through my closed curtains, In Charge said "Good morning, David. How was your night?" "Not so great" I puffed in reply. 'That should make her enquire more if she even heard and understood me,' I thought. "Oh, I'm sorry. Why was that?"

Reversing a Tsunami

Earlier in the day I'd just been given an extended discharge date of the 26th of May and should have been buzzing with this achievement. Instead, this particular day in mid-March I was thinking of only one thing: I took communion for the first time since Saturday the 2nd of November.

Though I was nil-by-mouth, so no bread, the chaplain was able to wipe the communion wine on my lips. Sam and I sobbed, and I struggled for breath as my emotional lability kicked in and my body spasmed. Forget thoughts of the inside of my car door to control it, I wanted to dwell on the mercy I believe was shown in the crucifixion of Jesus and that I believed was unfolding in my recovery. So sweet, so undeserved, so unfathomable. I'd written about it, believed I'd experienced it to a certain extent, but now its floodgates had been opened against the devastating tsunami of my strokes and it was turning the tide back. I believe I'd been allowed to survive the strokes to tell people about such mercy and it was worth straining every fibre and sinew of my being to be able to do that.

Thirteen
Pain Is My Friend

The youth group I pastored years ago in Loudwater, High Wycombe, had in it a scrawny lad who always got affectionately roughed up by the bigger lads. He would rise from the malaise of the bundle, arms aloft in fake victory, red-faced and unkempt, declaring, "Pain is my friend!" Mercifully, I seemed to be rising in genuine victory from a bundle with death, unkempt in real pain and discomfort all the time. Reluctantly pain was my friend.

There were two types of pain: Good pain and bad pain. Good pain really hurts, but I was in control of its intensity by my activity levels and medication. I also understood why it was occurring, so I could handle its presence. Good pain was caused by muscle weakness such as I was experiencing in my right shoulder for example. I knew from my teenage weight training days that you get lots of good pain when you undertake regular exercise. But this time, coming out of paralysis and doing so much exercise, everything was hurting all the time.

I include in this definition of good pain, discomfort. I had a lot of that. Untoned, inflexible, heavy weak muscles in my inactive limbs were being forced to move after neuroplasticity had repaired connections to my brain. I was constantly exploring what I could and couldn't do, relentlessly pushing the boundaries of what my body could take, so my days were full of discomfort.

Bad pain is when you're out of control of it and don't know why it's being generated – and nor does a consultant. Investigations are needed to find out why there's pain before something can be done. It's that sharp, searing pain that draws an intake of breath, that is comparable to giving birth or breaking a limb.

This Daddy Became a Mummy

In simple terms, I felt like an Egyptian mummy coming back to life. You're going to be a bit stiff after thousands of years of stillness. Though in my case it was only three to five months before most of my limbs started to have little movements. I was told I would still need months, maybe even years, of stretching and movement because the muscles and ligaments had been set in particular positions through paralysis.

There were bed sores through lack of movement, my face had to be awkwardly squeezed through T-shirts each day, and it goes without saying that I was a human pin cushion with all types of needles stuck in me. I never felt any pain in the first few weeks after the strokes because of the sedation, and I'm not sure I would have anyway given the total paralysis. But as neuroplasticity occurred and feeling was returning I was welcomed to a world of movement and pain.

None of this made me self-pitiful though. I was aware of it crouching at my door every day, but what good would it have done me to let it in? My life's purpose had been clarified and everything seemed to be working together for my good. I found great comfort in knowing there was purpose in my pain, but I can only imagine the sheer awfulness of pain without knowing its purpose.

I first encountered good pain at night in late January for five nights in a row. They were the most painful, uncomfortable, and disorientating nights of my life. The pain started directly after I began to self-correct during my early sitting balance physio sessions, coupled with my starting nightly sit-up attempts. I knew why I had it and just had to ride it out.

I awoke in the midnight hours to mild pain in my stomach area. Within an hour I was writhing with pain only I had no muscle strength to writhe. I managed to grab Jolly Dancer's attention and asked him to get help to reposition me on to my side instead of flat on my back. I'd spent the last hour with pain building up in my sides and spreading to my back and I was fantasising about the relief I should feel in my back and sides with my knees bent up towards my chest in a foetal position.

Jolly Dancer and another carer took a few minutes to move me trying to limit the pain but eventually I was on my side for the first time since the strokes. What I hadn't bargained for was the crushing effect of my internal organs on my breathing because I was slowly coming out of paralysis internally too. The muscles were untoned and gave no support to hold my lungs in place. It was bizarrely in that moment I realised why I had been on life support: my diaphragm's connection to the brain had been blocked by the clot making my muscles unable to help me breathe.

Initial relief gave way to gasping for breath and wincing with pain for about five minutes. Then Jolly Dancer and his colleague moved me to the other side. Mild relief ensued but it soon became a struggle to breathe again, and the pain remained. Defeated, I just got them to move me onto my back again and I saw out the night moaning and groaning with pain.

By the third night of this I begged them to hoist me into my wheelchair. Initially they refused out of confusion, but I begged all the more because I experienced little pain during the daytime, and I figured the upright position was helping. Indeed, it did help. I slept like a baby for five hours in my reclined chair and then Baritone got me back in bed for the day staff to wash and change me.

When I explained to new in post Cobbler what was going on at nights and why I was so tired in our sessions, she just said "You should ask for Ibuprofen." Of course, why had I not thought of that? From suffering sciatica the previous year I knew it reduced swelling in muscle tissue thus giving relief. The truth was I experienced such pain those nights and was delirious from tiredness I wasn't thinking straight. It seriously relieved the problem - but what a week of 'good' pain that was.

The Most Beautiful Shoulder in the World

An example of the discomfort I faced daily was when I'd wake up each morning aware of the feeling of a vice-like grip around the right side of my jaw, keeping my whole mouth virtually shut. After the trachea was taken out I'd spend the first half hour of the morning struggling for breath whilst hurriedly trying to stretch my jaw open a bit so I could breathe more easily because my nose was always blocked. If I sneezed my jaw and teeth would lock almost closed again.

I quickly had to learn as well to concentrate on keeping my tongue out the way of my teeth when sneezing or having a morning involuntary spasm. Safe to say, when I woke, I had to be wide awake immediately for self-preservation's sake.

The bad pain I discovered in my left shoulder in Lewisham from Wipey's spontaneous physio hadn't gone and left me wincing some mornings if the carers weren't careful enough putting my arm through a sleeve. When they got me into position for the various transfer aids before lifting both my shoulders felt they were being pulled out of their sockets. Every session Task Master did started with her trying to 'stretch out' the pain carefully – but it only worked for my right shoulder. In early February, our ward consultant came to my bedside to diagnose the problem. My left shoulder would need Botox injections.

A female physio administered the Botox injection and as she pulled the needles out of my left shoulder she said, "There you go, you've got the most beautiful left shoulder in the world now!" The bad pain reduced dramatically over the weeks, and I was told exercise and pain killers should do the rest as they were doing for my right shoulder.

Whilst getting used to the awkwardness of right-hand only living for the time being, something weird was going on with my left arm. Not only was it too heavy to lift but also had 'tone' in the left bicep extending into the forearm. This always made my left arm look bent as if I were holding my arm across my tummy, but I wasn't doing anything. It didn't stop me from trying to straighten it though, but the 'tone' of the forearm made it jolty when I did and there was severe restriction too. When I relaxed the arm, immediately after it would clam back up into its resting position. All these niggly little things mounted up with all my other symptoms to make life extremely painful on occasion and very uncomfortable which ground me down at times.

I'm on Pause

My pain and discomfort was difficult for Sam because there wasn't much she could do to alleviate it. But she could help treatment along and make me comfortable. She used to massage my face, stretch out my hamstring, wipe away my dribble, and cut my nails. That last one was more crucial than it sounds because on occasion when I sneezed my left-hand clawed up and drew blood. She even picked my nose each day after the trachea came out to help me breathe – gross. I was just so needy and dependent with everything. I often said to her, "You're the best nurse."

Pain was my friend because it was so common, but also because its gradual reduction helped me chart my progress. It was also a reminder that there was a time I couldn't feel anything including pain, not even anything, so there was part of me that was grateful to be able to feel pain.

In the meantime, I had to go through all this daily discomfort, heaviness, random full-body shakes, and pain. I had to handle incredible levels of self-consciousness and watch my family deal with a new disabled father, husband, son, and brother. I asked Sam a few times if she felt she'd lost her husband, she just smiled with relief and said "David, I'll take this over death any day." Sobering, but I took her point. I'd reassure her saying, "I'm just on pause."

Poo Bum Wee

When Sophie and Samuel were young they both went through phases where they'd regularly manage to turn discussions to their new-found fascination with all things disgusting. It got so out of hand that before we said 'grace' for our evening meal I'd half-jokingly, half-seriously say in a loud voice "Right, no poo bum wee at the table!" We'd all innocently laugh because it sounded like a South Asian name lost in translation, but they got the message: no toilet talk. And it worked… for about two minutes.

Therefore I will spare you from a detailed analysis of a key period of a few weeks around the end of February. But briefly, I started to be able to pick my own nose (much to Sam's relief) and survive early morning breathing struggles myself, to have my catheter out in preference for a bottle, and majestically began to use the toilet again for 'number two's' instead of my nappy. The whole few weeks were one big 'Don't get excited but…' moment too gross to mention.

Rehab became about my waterworks for those few weeks in late February and involved many different females intricately negotiating my private parts with hitherto unknown accuracy inside and out, which was painfully embarrassing at first. It was all in a day's work for the carers but because I was a long way off mastering my new 'car door' thought life, every moment of it was painfully embarrassing because of my spontaneous displays of inappropriate and unbridled laughter.

It would have been nice if those two Australian speech and language therapists who first saw me in intensive care had said something different than they had like, "We've been sent in to try and establish communication with you. You're in St Georges hospital, Intensive Care Unit, London. You've had a brain stem stroke – oh, and by the way, for the next ten months you're going to lose your dignity multiple times each day and night." That would have been helpful, but I don't think even that would have prepared me for these two weeks the details of which are thankfully consigned to the annals of history. For some reason though, hanging naked in a swinging sling whilst peeing like a garden cherub is forever seared onto my conscience.

It hit me after the kerfuffle of those few weeks had died down that if I'd not sorted out those toileting issues before my current discharge date of the 26th of May, Sam would have had to help out at home somehow. Yes I would have had local authority carers, but they wouldn't always be there when needed. That would have certainly brought new depths to our marriage. I wasn't sure how I felt about that, it would probably be gross for Sam and humiliating for me. I thought about the reality of that scenario for a moment, maybe inevitable in old age but I couldn't quite imagine it at our age. Of course, what I had forgotten about in that pensive moment was the pressing need to develop enough strength, balance, and skill needed to wipe my own backside...

Dark Times

Physical pain is one thing but the psychological pain I experienced was totally different and all-consuming at times. Thinker was on call for all the patients and was a busy man. Everyone was dealing with psychological issues of one sort or another, whether they knew it or not. A sudden brain injury leading to a life altering condition is hard to swallow at the best of times.

For me, the psychological acceptance process began in intensive care with my fleeting thoughts of 'This is happening,' mercifully made easier by hearing "You're going to be okay" from The Voice. I would immediately try and move a limb (unsuccessfully) to confirm it to myself that I was paralysed. Throughout that week I tried to get up a few times but the lack of response from my limbs confirmed the fact I was paralysed. I was just too sedated to start processing it properly though.

Two major issues were settled in that first week: how my purpose in life was going to be affected by this and that I still believed that the God of my youth was as merciful as I'd just written about before the strokes. Firstly, my life at last made sense. I could see how this event would enhance my message of mercy. It was immeasurably more than all my expectations to have such power working in my body so as to recover from something this devastating. All confusion and frustration about my calling that had dogged me in my adult life immediately left me and I just basked in the newfound peace of His plan for my life. The conclusiveness of this first answer only confirmed my strength of belief in Him.

Whilst in Maple Ward, those divine words spoken to me back in St George's kept me so calm and were bubbling away inside me like a brook. It just wouldn't stop. I didn't have to try to believe them, rather I couldn't not believe them because they became more overwhelming than my condition. I never felt I was in one of the most shockingly horrific medical states of being trapped in my own body so I can't resonate with others I've since heard of who have been and describe it as such.

Now in Putney I found myself collecting thoughts together of my experience so far. Being one hundred percent dependent on others for everything every day regarding my existence, even for my very breath, I felt like I was being divinely taught about mercy first hand. Mercy is for those who recognise they're in need. We are all in need every day even for the breath of life, but life has a way of insulating us from this awareness. A salary, friendships, and good health for example, can make us feel like we're not in need, but none of those put breath in our body. We are all living on mercy.

There was one question I had all along: "*How* was I going to be okay?" I was not being told this but was discovering the answer gradually during my stay. I was learning what it looked like, what it felt like, how I was being perceived, how long it was going to take, and what I thought about myself throughout. I felt these were things that I'd learn over and over especially when I went home.

I've known a lot of people in life who are of faith or of none who ask through their own dark times, "Why do bad things like this happen to a good person like me? What have I done to deserve this?" but it never arose in my mind. At the point I believe I encountered God powerfully in my bedroom in my early teens, I was convicted of my utter impurity before Him and recognised there was nothing good in me next to His goodness. As I look back now I believe His mercy has been following me everywhere since then.

In a group session at Putney they told me I'd suffered a life-altering event. I thought about that phrase a lot. I arrived at the thought that my life had not been altered by the strokes like they were trying to tell me it had. Yes it had been altered physically, in the short-term at least, and Sam and I were already having 'heart-to-hearts' about that. In the immediate term we were considering how this might affect the renovations and budget of our new home. The strokes had affected Sophie and Samuel mentally and they were both fumbling around trying to grapple with that in different ways. My strokes would alter where we were all living, and Samuel's schooling would be most affected by this. My journey through life had definitely been altered in terms of my expectations of the path I thought my life would take.

However, my life's purpose had not been altered. I lived to communicate to others in word and deed about the God who I believed in, in particular His mercy. This had altered my life more than the strokes. The strokes had served to enhance my purpose and was already finding expression in motivating me to get well.

We Don't Talk Anymore

One of my first dark times was not when I was locked-in, as you may have thought, but it started about fifteen minutes after one of my most joyous times – when my trachea was taken out. Sam and I were having pent-up tears of relief that a real milestone in my recovery had passed. I could now say "I love you" without blinking.

But shortly after we'd composed ourselves, the state of my mouth and jaw, along with the condition of my facial muscles came crashing down on me. On top of that was the awareness of dysarthria. Such a glorious moment was muted so quickly. Understandably depression sunk in almost immediately. I sulked for about two weeks. So much was wrong with me. It just crushed me, and I needed time to process it and galvanise myself into some kind of constructive response.

In the following couple of weeks I just found myself grunting at people because it was so hard to talk, and I couldn't be bothered to put in the effort because I was trying so hard with every other area of my body. Sam even had to revert to the alphabet board a few times again because my speech was so unclear.

Forget the purpose of my life revolving around communication, I was down because I didn't have it even just for basic communication. What was worse was Giggle couldn't offer me any hope. I could tell she wanted to, but she couldn't preserve her professional integrity any other way. I wanted her to say, "Don't worry David, this is common and usually goes away after a few weeks." But all she could say was "Everyone's different..." I had no medical guarantees and the assuring words bubbling around inside me didn't explain how or when I'd get better.

Then one day Giggle was wheeling me back to my bedside after a session I had been pretending to engage with. We were quite a way off and on a different floor, so we had to go via a lift. It had a big square mirror she parked me in front of. I tried to smile at myself to see if it looked as weird as it felt. Only the left corner of my mouth moved. I tried with all my might to smile the other side of my mouth but there was minimal movement and it felt so uncomfortable and heavy.

Then something just clicked in my head. 'If it's going to take this much effort to pull a half smile then that's what it'll have to take.' No more pretending in sessions, no more grunting and groaning, I was committed to putting in the effort to do something about it. I had no choice but to do what I could do. I didn't want to live like this, so I was going to do all within my power to maximise the mercy I'd been given.

There were sometimes when thoughts just got on top of me: 'How would I play the guitar again with a claw hand?' and 'Would I ever feel my left ankle again?' or 'Would I ever have sex again?' But these thoughts wouldn't come one by one at different times, they'd build up internally throughout the day and then be sitting there ready for me after rehab sessions had finished.

I wouldn't want to see anyone in those times except Sam. One time my parents came to see me, and I made them wait outside the room for half an hour or so. After a while I felt I had to let them in to visit but I was glum and non-engaging. It obviously set Mum off as she stood up abruptly saying "I can't do this anymore" and walked out. It took that experience to make me realise how my situation was wearing on others. I'd become so wrapped up in my body and the implications of it for living that I was paying no attention to how others were being affected. I felt thoughtless – not very good for a vicar. My parents were a constant source of comfort and encouragement to me, but it was draining on them. Everyone has their breaking point. It made me want to start saying sorry to everyone, but as people rightly pointed out to me, I had nothing to say sorry for. I hadn't asked for the strokes but was becoming more aware of how they were impacting others.

Darker Than Darkness

One day I was in my one-handed wheelchair when Task Master asked if I wouldn't mind having my photo taken for her records "Of course" I said without a second thought. When her phone clicked a thought crossed my mind 'I don't mind being pictured as disabled.' My daily routine meant the fact of being disabled was not lost on me but as she took it my mind wandered onto the process I was going to have to go through to be okay again.

I was wondering about my recovery, why and how people were treating me, and how long it might take. I became very pensive afterwards. I realized there were going to be a few years at least where I would be officially disabled. My thoughts wrangled with the fact that even though I still didn't consider myself disabled I was. I was becoming more accepting of this phase now, not that I hadn't accepted it before, but it was becoming more real for me and the family.

These situations were emotional and difficult to process, but nothing compared to my first and most notable dark time earlier in the month. It was the darkest moment of my life, and it occurred on the 4th of February.

It was early morning and everything was dark and still. My trachea had recently been taken out and I was well and truly on a fight back to normal. I had just galvanised myself to deal with my talking situation so you would have thought I'd be feeling positive. But I'd been lying awake for some time now and was thinking about all that was wrong with me. Apart from my left eyelid, right foot, and vital internal organs nothing else worked properly. I didn't understand a lot of what and why my body was the way it was at that time. I became confused and didn't understand how things would work out. I was being tossed about in another tsunami wave.

It had taken a little over three months, but I finally decided I didn't want 'this' anymore. I couldn't live like it, and I couldn't bear the situation any longer. The Voice wasn't bubbling away inside me that morning. It wasn't that I was doubting His words, but it seemed there were just no words to doubt – like they had never been spoken. I felt empty and full of hopelessness. Vacuous darkness seemed to swirl around inside of me emptying me of reason and swallowing me up. It was a darkness I'd never known before. It was indefinably massive as it swept over me and consumed my very soul and emotions with nothingness. I felt lonely, isolated and… abandoned.

I had no answers for it and no explanation. I wasn't able to reason it away because it seemed entirely justifiable based solely on my condition as it was. Then I thought a thought I could never imagine myself thinking for the first and only time in my life 'Why don't I kill myself and end it all?' The thought of being immediately free from all suffering sucked me in. I entertained it and moved closer to it, ready to embrace it. Huff Puff's erroneous assessment back in Lewisham was now correct – I had given up the will to live.

Then a moment of rationalisation hit me: 'How am I going to do it?' I couldn't move, and I was living in a place where they specialised in keeping people alive. 'Hopeless' I thought, 'The one time I want to commit suicide and I can't even do that – pathetic.' Looking back it was a mercy, but at the time it compounded things even more if that were possible.

Just then Musical Gangster walked past my door for the morning team meeting "Hey Dave, how ya doin?" He'll never know what he jolted me out of. Glancing at the clock I remember thinking 'That seemed like forever,' but it was only five minutes. Still long enough though to get lost in my lostness.

I was so annoyed with myself for being so selfish and losing all perspective. What about Sam? What about Sophie? What about Samuel? I would have caused them so much more heartache. There were signs of hope with every limb and organ of my body that I'd just lost sight of and our new life in Surrey was shaping up nicely.

Later that day I confessed all to Sam because we tell each other everything. I said I didn't want to cause her any worry but was just making her aware that I was that vulnerable. Not saying a word she just held the back of my hand in comfort. I could tell she knew the same aloneness from her perspective. Without speech or blinking we were communicating on a deeper level.

I would think about that experience a lot over the coming weeks. As a Baptist minister it had a profound effect on me. That yearly reminder of the death of Jesus on Good Friday is characterised by Jesus' cry "My God, my God, why have you forsaken me!" even though He knew He was going to be okay. I now knew a sip of that reality. I could relate to something now that had eluded me all my life. It wasn't a cry of doubt but the awful desperation of separation. Out of my suffering was coming a new divine acquaintance, a divine knowing.

How Would I Get Better?

The answer to this recurring question buzzing round my mind in those early months was being revealed throughout these dark times. I was figuring out slowly, experience by experience, how I was going to recover. I was going to have to work my way out of it and rediscover my competitive edge again – this time not against others but against myself. It was going to take a long time and we definitely weren't going to Cyprus.

I had been shaped and formed throughout life to be the way I was for such a time as this. It would be challenging, it would be painful, it would sometimes be dark and lonely, but my faith was being revealed for what it was – genuine. Mine and Sam's love for each other was being taken to depths I didn't even know existed. I had an all-encompassing knowing that even in the darkest of times I'd be okay.

Fourteen
What in the World

What in the world could possibly stop the rehab that was helping me from continuing to recover so well… a global pandemic that's what.

I got a rude awakening from my recovery bubble I'd been in when I watched on television as repatriated British citizens from Wuhan, China, were being bussed from RAF Brize Norton to NHS staff accommodation at Arrowe Park Hospital, the Wirral, to 'isolate.' 'That looks serious,' I thought, and from then on Covid-19 was a thing.

It was the topic of conversation on everyone's lips. We were all waking up to the severity of the virus and visiting protocols were introduced to limit the risk of it spreading. But within just over a month the World Health Organisation had labelled it a pandemic.

Locked-Down but Not Locked-In

By this time there was widespread talk of a national lockdown which seemed unthinkable at the time, but Putney struck first taking us all by surprise. Sam appeared as usual at noon on Saturday the 15th of March with the kids in tow. They were all crying.

"We've been told at 7pm tonight there will be no more family visits allowed for the foreseeable future. The hospital's going into self-imposed lockdown" Sam cried. I was shocked as it was the first I'd heard about it. Playing the role of dad for the first time in a long time I said calmly "Let's get back to the room" where I tried to reassure them. Practical realities distracted me enough so my lability could make nothing of the sadness I felt.

We were blindsided by this and the gradual emotional upward curve we had all been experiencing with my recovery was thrown into disarray. All the emotional support I was getting from the whole family was going to go virtual until my discharge on the 26th of May and the closeness we all felt was under threat. Sam and I had only ever been apart for a few weeks once in our twenty-seven years of marriage. I couldn't yet operate my phone, so I was going to have to learn quick. I was forced to take another step towards independence but I'd rather it had not been under these circumstances.

I steered them towards the positives for Sam: She would now be able to start a phased return to her job by working from home which in turn would enable her to oversee the building renovations to our new home. She could still be involved in my recovery by doing my washing. It helped a bit, but that evening was a long drawn-out 'goodbye.' Sam's diary entry for that final day was just a long black horizontal line severing the page indicating 'The End.' They were uncertain times for our family again.

When the whole nation was locked down the next week we had to think practically. We managed to get a letter from my consultant to confirm our renovations were essential for my return home at the end of May. While all construction work down our road ceased, mercifully ours continued under social distancing regulations.

What didn't continue but slowly faltered was the therapy sessions. We heard that the virus was in the building and therapists were reassigned to cover carer's duties who were dropping like flies to the virus. All staff started doing extra shifts to cover the shortfall and agency staff we didn't know started appearing. A 'war effort' spirit prevailed and everyone was just so appreciative of others as they all mucked in. Putney stopped functioning as a rehabilitation facility and just operated as a hospital.

Just after everyone was ordered to 'Stay at home' in the UK I unexpectedly received a letter saying all patients were to be discharged as soon as possible for safety reasons. The intention was that after the virus had passed we would return and finish our allotted rehabilitation times. We were both shocked. I was in no condition to go home because I still needed round the clock care. I was assured there was a care package of four visits a day being put in place for me. Sam was alarmed at me going home to a building site in my condition and at having to keep me alive. She would be given socially distanced training on how to administer my medications, food and water through my peg and she began taking deliveries of supplies immediately. The reality of living with severe disability at home started to sink in and I didn't like it. Our shock was slightly eased when we were both told this could all take up to four weeks to arrange.

Making the Best of It

As I thought about the positives of my situation they began mounting up: the virus not in our ward, I could still exercise, I could do unlimited amounts of standing on the Rotunda (a home-based transfer aid the NHS was giving me) when I eventually got home, but best of all I'd be with Sam and Samuel. In every church, job, or property renovation I'd always experienced unexpected problems and learnt the best way to deal with it is focus and work with the positives, and my recovery was to be no different. Up till now I'd been making steady progress but now there was something in the world that was trying to hinder me, so I had to do something about it.

Night-time exercises continued and helpfully Task Master left me with equipment to carry on her routines in the day-time. We were confined to the ward so I could also do circuits of the ward in my wheelchair. And I developed two key exercises to help improve my quality of life. The first was for my left leg. I couldn't pull it back up onto my wheelchair foot plate if my overactive quads sprung it off. It only needed to be lifted a few centimetres up and back, but I couldn't even do that. I set myself the challenge of sliding it off its foot plate and lifting it back on with no help from my right hand. Each day I would strain with all the effort in my body until out of breath. Perhaps once every fifteen minutes I would manage it – other times I'd have to lift it back up with my right hand.

Big Money, fighting his own boredom by answering work emails for his construction company, once joked with me "What are you doing – dancing?" I just laughed and carried on but in my head I answered, 'No, I'm trying to get better.' I wondered if I was showing him up but if I'd have had no neuroplasticity in my entire left-side like him would I be bothering?

The second exercise was bending down to try and touch my toes. Fighting the fear of falling forwards and enduring good stretching pain, I got lower and lower as the weeks went on. I had to push my dead-weight of a left arm out the way so I could go further. Sitting back up helped my back strength too. The day I managed to touch my shoelaces was memorable. 'Hello laces, I haven't been in touch with you for six months' I thought. It was a great moment to tell Sam about on video call.

Now there was time to fill I got involved in the war effort and started doing my own personal care in the mornings, freeing up the carers to move on to the next patient. It was a struggle, took an inordinate amount of time and left me out of breath, but in her absence I knew I was making Task Master proud.

In one of our daily video calls I told Sam of a glorious mistake Musical Gangster made. In his rush between patients because of low staff numbers he lowered me down from the Cyra Steady onto a proper toilet with no commode or disabled arm bars. He realised when it was too late, "Oh no, you okay man?" I smiled excitedly and tongue in cheek replied, "This is cool man." I had never been so excited to sit on a normal loo.

Tour Guide was also making the best of it by delivering random physio sessions. He spontaneously appeared at my bedside one afternoon. He said excitedly with a grin, "I thought we'd try this." I was surprised but elated. It was the last transfer aid there was, called the Red Return. It is basically a red iron sack barrow that I was to stand on with no side bars or straps to stop me toppling, and nothing to sit on, when a carer would transfer me. I passed his strength tests with flying colours, so he showed the carers how I was to use it safely on the ward because my left hand and quads wouldn't playing ball.

Bus Driver was still using it, as he had been when I first moved into our room, and Big Money wasn't as successful as me with it. I felt a bit embarrassed as I'd caught up one neighbour and overtaken the other. But a good camaraderie existed between us now and they gave me great encouragement, putting me at ease.

The Virus Is in the Ward

Mother's Day came and went breaking up the boredom of weekends. It was the first time I'd not been at home for it. Although it wasn't called 'Wife Day' it should have been – Sam was a special lady. I used to say that to her often and these past few months had shown it once again. This ordeal was stretching her emotional, mental, and spiritual capacity to what we thought was the maximum. Samuel and Sophie had been totally pampering her and had stepped up without my prompting and done me proud, confirming to me that my role as a father was changing not just because of my strokes but because of their age.

Those four exercise filled weeks dragged on as I waited for my discharge. Downing Street briefings got more solemn whilst safety procedures at Putney got ever stricter, confining us to our rooms. I had no Therabite for my jaw, could only stand for a few seconds each day when being transferred and could no longer wheel around the ward. I was constantly asking nurses to wipe transfer aids down and wash their hands before attending to me, trying to avoid catching the virus. I was coming into close contact with so many carers at that time I was starting to feel vulnerable.

It became my habit to wheel myself to the door of our room a few times each day so I could at least get a change of view and see human activity. As the carers walked by they would always ask "How are you, David?" "Bored" would come my standard reply. But one day something caught my eye which unnerved me. It was a new red sign above a door to another room with big white capital letters on it reading ISOLATION. "Has somebody in the ward got the virus?" I asked a passing nurse. "Yes, three patients have it." The virus was now in Drapers Ward. I was glad I was going home soon 'I'll be safe there' I thought.

Tuesday the 8th of April was the penultimate day before my discharge arrived, and it would be an understatement to say that after weeks of boredom and waiting I was ready to go home, excited to see the family in-person again. But little did I know that Sam, Sophie, and Samuel's capacity was about to be stretched even further.

"Do you feel hot, David?" asked the carer doing my observations that morning. "Now you mention it, I do feel a bit hot. Can you open the window?" Since the brain stem stroke my temperature regulation had been affected. "I'll just go and let someone know" she said. 'Someone' I thought, 'Who? Why?'

She returned almost immediately saying words I'll never forget in a too obviously calm way "The next people you're going to see will be dressed strange, but don't worry." 'Don't worry' I thought. Immediately, looking like Marty McFly out of the film Back to the Future, three people (who I'd never seen before) with full-bodied plastic white aprons and yellow head gear with full-face plastic visors, masks and gloves appeared. "Hello David, we're just going to move you, your bed, and all your belongings immediately to the isolation room." Then they said that tried and tested sure fire way to get you worried "Don't worry."

I video called Sam from that lonely room keeping her abreast of things as the day unfolded. At one point when I told her I'd just taken a Covid swab she paused, took a deep breath, then with a controlled tone said "Okay. What's happening about tomorrow?" I couldn't tell her because I didn't know, but it wasn't looking good.

That night my temperature raged. I awoke in pools of water and sticky sheets. Baritone said in his deep Congolese accent "I don't like your temperature reading, Dave." It was 38.1 degrees. I knew it was the virus and that meant I wasn't going home anytime soon – my heart sunk. How would I tell Sam? I could say 'Don't get excited but... my temperature regulation is getting better!' Somehow I knew that wasn't going to cut it.

First thing in the morning before I'd had time to ring Sam, dressed as Marty McFly's the carers and Tour Guide moved me into a single isolation room. I waited in the empty Day Room masked up for the first time, but mistakenly without any water rigged up as normally happened each morning. The move took a couple of hours because of new procedures. After all that time, having sweated all night and not having the fluids replaced, I started to feel a little faint when alone in my new room.

I reached for the call bell, but it wasn't on my bed where it usually was. I remember turning my head round to start wheeling myself to the door to shout for help, when suddenly I felt life draining out of my body and being replaced with heaviness – just like the onset of my strokes. I couldn't lift my arms to wheel myself to the door let alone grip the shiny rims. Somehow I managed to get enough purchase on the tyres themselves and put in two pushes. I glided slowly to an awkward halt against the door frame and moaned softly with bowed head "Help me."

From my point of view this is what happened next: Blurred vision, closing darkness, loud beeping, running feet, panic. Male voices shouting, hoist squeezed under me. Hoist whirring noise. 'Ah, soft bed.' Sharp pain in the back of my left hand. Sleep.

I'd fainted through dehydration and spent the next two days on IV fluids. I woke up to find I'd been asleep since about 11am and it was now 6pm. I felt great, it was the best sleep I'd had since the strokes. Full of oxygen from a tank pumped in through my nose, fed and watered and on a catheter. But best of all, no temperature – the drama was over. It was Wednesday evening.

The next day I was wheeled off for a chest x-ray. They were doing everything they could to confirm whether I had Covid-19 or not. I looked at the x-ray screen as they took the picture of my lungs and I saw it – the deadly virus killing tens of thousands in this country and millions around the world, causing whole nations to economically dive, and making ghost towns of city centres. In the bottom of my right lung was an area of what appeared to be white netting showed up on the screen. 'That's it, that's what's stopping world economies.'

For me to live the white netting had to recede but for me to die it was going to have to spread. The latter didn't correspond with what I believed about my recovery though. It didn't make sense to have survived the strokes, to be experiencing such a remarkable recovery, having my life's purpose affirmed, only to be fatally struck down by the virus. That's what I told Sam when I was eventually able to phone her the next day.

Death and Resurrection

Sophie had come home from university so the family could all be together if the worst happened, therefore I kept them up to date three times daily with my temperature readings to reassure them – they never went above 36.9C. I had no symptoms after that first sweaty night. The swab test result came back positive confirming the x-ray and Sam told all my friends on Facebook that I had Covid-19, though by then I felt I was over the worst of it.

The long countdown had begun to when I would see Sam again after two weeks of isolation. I did no exercise that first week preserving my strength for fighting the virus. Time passed slowly of which I was regularly reminded from the news channels I had on the television. The door could only be slightly ajar and people interaction was kept to a minimum. For the first few days it was really difficult because I was unable to wheel about, being rigged up to IV fluids, and felt like I was seizing up. I wasn't locked-in anymore, but I might have well been.

I found it was much better to focus on listening prayer than on endless television news about death, death, death. But just before I decided to turn it off there was a report about people complaining about being locked down. 'Try being locked in' I thought. People were only moaning about being stuck in their homes. 'But you've got other rooms' I'd retort. Then the report focussed on a stressed single mum stuck in a high-rise flat with two kids. 'But you've got two working legs to walk around in it and you're not alone' I retorted.

It was harsh and was virtue signalling at its best. I felt I had a right to say these things because no-one had had it worse than me these past few months. But I didn't like what was being revealed in me. My heart was being refined even there amongst such suffering, with hidden realms of pride and selfishness being brought to the surface that were hitherto unknown.

There were people here worse than me now. Some had no feeling down one side of their body, some patients had lost their cognitive functions, some were long-term patients with no hope of ever going home. Apart from the mounting virus deaths and grieving families, what about soldiers who'd lost limbs in combat? What about those affected by thalidomide? What about cancer suffers? What about those tortured for their faith under oppressive regimes?

I was humbled. Suffering is relative. In intensive care I had been worse off than most, but not now mercy was unfolding in me, the therapists had worked their magic, and Sam's love and that of my family was strengthening me. It was a lesson learnt.

When I did watch television it wasn't the news anymore it was just daytime television all day which was mind numbingly boring, apart from the odd property show. Beamer popped his head round the door once and caught me watching them "Ah, Mr David! You like property? I need a house." Whenever he popped his head round the door he would always ask for house buying tips after I told him my background.

I can't emphasise enough just how long and boring that first week seemed. At one point I even caught myself intently studying the different shades of yellow caused by refraction in my catheter bag. I may also have gone to the loo a few more times than I needed to just so I could have some activity and stand a bit. There was one hilarious moment though that broke up the boredom spectacularly. A chirpy physio from another ward offered to play a game of large A4 cards with me to break up the boredom. At the end it suddenly dawned on both of us that she'd have to laboriously disinfect all fifty-two cards individually.

By the second week I was sure the virus in my lungs had receded and I wouldn't have any resurgence – and so it proved to be. I had been the last patient in Drapers Ward to get the virus and fortunately our strain had only been very slight, but reports were coming in that other wards hadn't been so fortunate.

My focus that second week was about how to stave off the aching excitement of seeing Sam and the family again. I did this the only way I knew how – exercising. Task Master's dumbbell had not been transferred to my isolation room, so Sam had some delivered enabling me to restart my right-arm routine.

There were several milestones I reached that second week that helped fuel my continued optimism: I managed to scrape my shoes off one day, I gingerly wrote my name with my left hand using a biro and a tissue, and I also squeezed a few millimetres on my left hand clencher that Sam had bought.

But the crowning glory of that isolation period was on Easter Day. I was able to Zoom into Belvedere Baptist Church service on my phone, much to their surprise. It was the first time they'd seen me since I was taken from them so suddenly. I wanted to thank them for their prayers and care for my family and, as Easter Day is all about resurrection, it was kind of cool that I could make an appearance – after all, I'd had a resurrection of sorts. It gave me great hope that despite my dysarthria and facial problems, they could understand me. I was sure now that preaching again was possible.

Frantic Negotiation

On the Monday of the last week of isolation I woke up thinking 'I've made it.' I'd survived the virus, got through the boredom of the last two weeks, and I knew tomorrow was my last day by myself. On Wednesday I'd be going home and seeing Sam again but my excitement about that thought wouldn't last long.

Later that morning, Tour Guide and Task Master entered the room with sullen faces. "We've got some difficult news for you" they said. "Rehab is going to restart at fifty percent capacity, but we can't promise it'll increase. So if you go home it'll be seen as a rejection of what we're offering, and you won't be allowed back." I could tell they didn't want to give me the news and it was the last thing I wanted to hear – hopes dashed at the last again.

There followed a day of fraught video calls, phone calls, and discussions with all parties concerned about how I could go home but still come back when full physio started. But Putney weren't budging and nor could they when they had such a long waiting list. The virus was not going away any time soon and they, like everyone else, didn't know how it was going to affect their services long-term. Even if I'd not had the strokes we definitely wouldn't have made it to Cyprus – the whole world was in suspended animation.

The next day I was sharing my woes with Overseer when she said, "Why don't you ask for weekend leave, that way you can have the best of both worlds?" She said it so matter of fact. "Is that possible? Is that even a thing?" I asked. "David, we are a rehab facility. We'll do anything to accommodate your recovery and assimilation back into society." I was literally stunned.

Sam was shocked and beside herself with joy when I told her. It was as if scales fell from our eyes and a world of new possibilities opened up before us. I could see Sam and Samuel

(Sophie was back at University now), I could be involved in the renovations more (the builders worked on Saturdays), I could do loads of standing on the equipment delivered at home, and I could still have rehab back at Putney during the week.

Later that day Tour Guide came back needing to know what I was going to do. "I have a counter-offer for you." He laughed and rocked back on his chair with surprise, "You can't give me a counter-offer!" he exclaimed, clearly caught by surprise. "For almost four weeks the possibility's been dangling in front of me of being able to see Sam again, and for the second time that's been scuppered. Let me have weekend leave and I'll stay. Sam is already fully trained to administer my medication and food, and she's effectively isolated due to working from home." His brain ticked over "Give me a minute" he said, as he got up and left. Fifteen minutes later he was back. "The answer is 'Yes,' but infection control say you must agree to do a Covid swab test every Monday morning." I smiled with the left side of my face "Done!"

I had gone into isolation with Covid-19 and had come out doing proper weights on my right arm and with weekend leave secured at weekends. Something that could have been fatal at worst, or at best slowed my recovery, served to propel me forward. Good was coming out of this dark time. My previous discharge scheduled for May was scrapped because of the lost time to Covid-19 and I was given Friday the 3rd of July instead – Sam's birthday.

Those last few days of the week were filled with pure joy at how things had worked together for good. Anticipation built towards Friday when I'd see Sam again, see the whole family, get to ride in 'Black Shadow,' and get to see my new home for the first time. The rest of the week went very quickly but not before something significant happened.

Fight Back From Paralysis

The physio team was slowly returning, and they set up a temporary gym in the Day Room behind some wheeled screens, as the gym was still off limits. Cobbler was back after three weeks in bed with Covid, and we had time for one session together before I went home, but what a session it was.

She got me up walking alongside a plinth. Walking still didn't feel right and made me realise how far I had to go to reach my goal. I was downcast and almost tearing up. She realised how I was feeling about the session, sat down next to me and calmly said some words I've never forgotten. "David, when you arrived here four months ago you were locked-in and severely paralysed all over, just look how far you've come." It was a light bulb moment. She was right. I'd just staggered unaided along a plinth for goodness' sake. I'd come an awful long way. My fight back to normal was becoming demoralising, looking at how far I need to go, and she showed me how to keep up my motivation by tracking my recovery. My mindset needed to change. I wasn't on a fight back to normal anymore but on a fight back from paralysis. And let me tell you, I was going to get as far away from paralysis as I could. I was going home with a metaphorical spring in my step.

Fifteen
Weekend Leave

It was Friday morning the 24th of April, and I had butterflies. I was going to see Sam again after nearly six weeks of video calls. The carers packed my clothes, toiletries and medications for the weekend whilst at the same time moving the rest of my stuff into my new men's room dedicated for Covid-19 survivors. As Task Master and Tour Guide were coming to check I could function in my new home they wheeled me down towards the entrance. The anticipation built as I was pushed down the long, high corridors to the entrance. I started leaning forward as we got to reception to see if I could see Sam waiting in 'Black Shadow,'

There she was stepping out of the car. "Hellooo!" Sam cried with a big smile and outstretched arms. I tried not to cry but the floodgates opened when she bent down to hug me. My emotional lability kicked in and I started to howl and convulse but I didn't care. I could hold her with my right arm, smell her hair and feel our cheeks touching as we embraced. Though the threat of death had once again tried to separate us, we were together again.

Going Home to a New Home

Having just been the awkward bystanders in our private reunion Task Master and Tour Guide helped to transfer me from my wheelchair to 'Black Shadow.' Using the red return I lowered myself back into the car, Samuel sat in the driver's seat to stop me falling backwards whilst they swung my legs in. The car doors shut and there was silence, no-one knew what to say. My expectancy had always been that this day would come but when it finally materialised we were all just stunned – it had taken six months to get to this point. As we pulled out of the car park Sam said through tears "So many times I've cried coming out of here without you but now you're with me." There was joy and relief in her quivering voice.

The car journey home was uncomfortable to say the least. Being unused to seeing a drivers view, everything seemed so bright and fast as we drove out of London down the A3. With my driving glasses on, everything was crisp and sharp like normal but still something was wrong. Things just seemed to unnervingly appear in my vision leaving me feeling not quite 'in the car,' somewhat dulling my excitement. Roundabouts flung me against the passenger window because of my weak core with my left arm offering no resistance. The leather seats were no match for a soft wheelchair and after ten minutes I literally felt like I was sitting on a rock. I wondered whether I'd ever drive again but because of the trajectory of my recovery I couldn't rule it out. I found myself in the weird waiting space of in between paralysis and normality.

The streets became familiar and childhood memories were triggered, blocking out these thoughts. No longer the concrete streets of Belvedere but our beloved leafy Surrey. We had followed my calling around the Southeast all our lives, feeling a bit like missionaries. We had tried and failed several times to get back here but now out of tragedy was coming the fulfilment of a long-held dream and I found it hard to take in. I turned to Sam and said, "Do we actually live here?" She smiled "Yup. It's no longer a dream – we're finally back."

Parking outside our new home we eventually found the flattest place on the curb to get out of the car and transfer to my wheelchair. It was a precarious transfer again with bent backs and people leaning over each other. Due to the adverse camber of the pavement I felt like I was going to tip over when I finally sat in my wheelchair. That and the journey home made me realise there was a lot I was going to have to adjust to in normal life.

With all the fuss I'd not paid much attention to my new home. Sam was wanting my approval for her choice of home and was quite apprehensive. She needn't have worried. It was a two-bedroom bungalow with one bathroom, on a wide plot with plenty of space for a side extension and new entrance. Though the front garden was covered with heaps of rubble from the current renovations I could tell it was big enough to have off-street parking – which I'd just discovered I desperately needed.

As we got indoors the smell of an old property filled my nostrils and the abnormally wide hallway, good sized rooms, and old teak built-in wardrobes filled my gaze. When I saw with my own eyes how long the garden was for our rear extension I turned to Sam and simply said, "The girl's done good!" There was bags of potential.

Tour Guide and Task Master confirmed the house was suitable for basic functions with a wheelchair, then they left. I don't think they were as enamoured with the state of the property as I was, but the rubble and dust would pass, and it would make for a super family home. As they shut the door behind them we just looked at each other, stunned, and both said, "Don't get excited but… we're home!"

Locked In One Room

As it was the only decent room, we ironically spent the weekend sat in one room. Sam had been living in the kitchen for the whole of the first lockdown. I went from sitting in my wheelchair in isolation to sitting in my wheelchair all weekend in a kitchen – but this time we were together.

This and all succeeding weekends could be summed up in two words: 'chat' and 'standing.' Though I was on a high hospital bed and Sam was on a low bed settee we just chatted all night and all morning. I found a position on my electrical bed where I could breathe okay to speak for extended times and Sam would sit up, tea in hand. We'd smile whilst reminiscing about our childhoods in the area, plan the next week of building decisions to be taken, work out renovation budgets, and compare design ideas. To some that might seem stressful and unromantic, but we loved it because we felt like we were building a whole new life together. We often remarked "How long would that conversation have taken using the alphabet board?!"

Standing was all about gaining strength and practising balance to get me closer to my main goal of walking. Sam would push me in the wheelchair right up to the Rotunda which allowed me to stand freely in it whilst safely surrounded on all sides by the kitchen table, its own metal bars and my wheelchair. I did bouts of up to twenty minutes until my legs shook too much to stand. I couldn't talk and stand at the same time then because of the sheer effort it took to hold my frame up and balance free hand, so I watched television to escape the boredom and pain. 'Landing' back in my wheelchair to Sam's encouragement was the tonic I'd missed these past lockdown weeks. I probably should have rested more during these weekends but I was so energised to stand because it was my road to walking and seemed too good an opportunity to miss.

Mum and Dad, Big Sis and Dom with Sam's dad would pop by outside as restrictions allowed now they were neighbours. They all wanted to see how work was progressing on the house and how I was progressing week-by-week. Even in lockdown we felt so supported and I got a much-needed emotional boost. The only sadness was, like so many others throughout that time, I couldn't see Stu and Mark with his family because they lived just too far away – video chats with them continued.

Sophie was restricted to university but always video called us together, and Samuel was next door in his bedroom. He buried himself in online gaming as soon as he got his promised television in his room (as I knew he would). But it was his only way to make friends at his new school because online learning was enforced two weeks after starting there.

He didn't realise how remarkable he was, showing such courage in the most difficult of circumstances. He was outstanding in the way he supported Sam with the move and now around the house with jobs I'd have done. When the strokes hit he was only a boy, but by the time I started weekend leave a growth spurt ensured he was as tall as me with a deep voice. I was so proud of him showing such initiative and resilience throughout our ordeal. When I was locked-in I'd felt he was at the time of life where he needed me the most, but evidently the space and responsibility he gained through my absence had been what he really needed. I don't think I would have given him that if I had been around.

Back to Work

Getting ready that Monday morning was a relief of sorts for me. I'd managed to do a 'No.2' on Friday afternoon and had avoided the need over the weekend. I was spared the ignominy of Sam having to wipe my backside and so was she. Though tension came when trying to get me back in the car by ourselves with just Samuel to help us. We managed but it wasn't pretty. We were all tense and stressed trying to help me balance and not get hurt. But we all had a laugh when I 'landed' in the passenger seat with my trousers severely twisted and pulling down towards my thighs.

Much to his delight, Samuel had to grab the back of my tracksuit trousers and give me a 'wedgy.'

Now my new house in Surrey was home, Putney became like a place of work. My mindset was beginning to change. Sam was working at home whilst I worked at my rehab. Though still physically apart for weekdays, we were together again building our new life. We were met at 'work' by two smiling and waving physios who would help get me out of the car that first Monday back. I kissed Sam goodbye and they wheeled me back inside with a trolley for all my clean clothes that she'd washed over the weekend. I always used to get back to my bed bay well before my sessions started so as I was rested, I got straight to it and started doing my right arm occupational therapy routine with weights. It felt good to be back in the 'going to work' mindset.

My new men's room had the usual four bays but only three men at first. Opposite me was a retired, grey Aussie. He had accidentally had a nerve cut in a routine operation which seriously impeded his limb control – he had to sleep with weights on his arms and legs to hold them down. I'd seen him around before once in the corridor where with clenched fist he'd said, "Never give up!" A cranky person with a wicked sense of humour, Cranky and I got on well. Cranky was the only other patient I saw doing a bit of their own exercise.

My next-door neighbour was a white English mid-fifties man from the sports entertainment world. He'd had five brain operations and though he was stable now, had gradually descended into his current state of just about walking unsteadily with a stick with jerky limbs, eyesight problems, and a droopy left-sided face. He was single and was often shouting angrily on the phone to people whilst he was trying to sort out his new life post-rehab. That must have been nerve-racking, knowing he was going to live alone in that condition. One day he even shouted at a friend on his phone "I don't like who I've become!" which told me all I needed to know about Shouty's state of mind. He just sat sulking in his wheelchair a lot watching television.

Every patient had a story and by now I knew most of them. I had become more understanding of their stories and why people's bodies did what they did. I didn't need to focus on normality now for encouragement because all around me people's recovery stories were encouraging me. Remember Wobbly who'd inspired me with her walking on my first morning in Putney? She was here because one day whilst standing in a London bus queue with her mates a car suddenly ploughed into her. How tragic. I felt terrible for her yet inspired by her at the same time.

Fight Back from Paralysis

Though my left arm was good for hardly anything, I decided it was time to start my right arm occupational therapy routine on it. I knew from Task Master's daily sessions that it was getting stronger through using the arm support machine. First were front arm raises with which I could now just get a few millimetres of clean air between my wrist and the wheelchair armrest. I did a few lifts but had to finish the routine just tensing the shoulder. I realised it was going to take at least a few years to have a chance of restoring full arm movement.

I tried the bicep curl next again with no weights. I managed again to do three sets of ten repetitions, but they weren't full curls either by any stretch of the imagination and were made harder by its twisted nature. With my right bicep I was already smoothly curling a three-kilogram dumbbell, so there was a huge disparity between the two limbs still. I hadn't had a 'left-side affected' stroke, rather my whole body was affected but my left side was severely affected. Lastly, I tried repping my arm out to the side. It was similarly weak and I only managed to move it about two or three inches from my wheel for three sets of ten.

The level of weakness it was possible to be reduced to by paralysis struck me deeply again. Muscle that is so weak it can't even lift itself is something to behold. It literally felt like my arm was coming out of its shoulder socket causing me to wince. I had agreed seated bed washes with Overseer before my first weekend home and the only way I could move my left arm out the way to help was to use gravity – welcome Pendulum. I had to lean over to my left and swing it onto the bed sheets to gain some friction so that when I self-corrected to avoid toppling over it wouldn't swing back against my leg again. My life had been reduced to controlling weak limbs with gravity.

I actually stopped doing one exercise with my right-hand gripper, but only because I could now use the Therabite which was an exercise in itself considering how much I used it each day. The effect was that within months I started waking up in the morning with almost a totally open jaw.

The Real Burger Sauce

McDonalds drive-thru's were starting to open up, so my goal of eating a Big Mac was back on. Giggle started making up for lost time and moved me immediately off ice chips and straight on to yoghurts, three times per day, and at weekends. The sensation of real food on my tongue for the first time in seven months is almost indescribable – prickly and smooth all at the same time as my taste buds were suddenly stimulated back into life. A world of taste just moved dramatically close. Sam had a choice of yoghurts ready for me to choose from the next weekend of all my favourite types. I'm not sure but I may have had slightly more than one per meal. We were so happy to be able to say 'Grace' as a family at the tea table again, it meant such a lot to us even if it was only for yoghurts.

Sam only spent a few weekends of feeding me burger sauce through my peg before minced solid foods started to be introduced. I had to concentrate hard on my swallow, so while I ate, Sam and Samuel sat in silence as I closed my eyes – just like that man I saw on my first morning in the Day Room. I would have been encouraged by his recovery if I had known his story instead of being freaked out.

I was feeling so confident with my swallow on foods now that Giggle helped me race through the different levels of progressively more solid food until I ate my first meal of proper food. As she took my food order I remembered how Foodie from Lewisham used to stare at my 'nil-by-mouth' sign every morning, I wish she could have seen me now. I ordered Spanish chicken with rice and vegetables and every moment of it was delectable. It was ironically brought to me by Musical Gangster who I'd seen on my first morning at Putney taking someone else their food. I was brought back down to earth from my exhilaration as he put my bib on. It was necessary to save me from the messy disaster my restricted mouth opening could cause. Cranky had obviously had one too many hospital meals because he complained about the food as usual, but I was so pleased to have normal food it could have been cheese salad for all I cared, my least favourite food on the planet.

I was a little slower with drinks though. By the end of rehab I was still on slightly thickened fluids and a bonus with drinking again was that my throat couldn't handle the sharpness of fizzy drinks. Sam had always been on at me about my consumption levels, but I couldn't kick the habit for love nor money, yet now I was gloriously free.

From the moment I swallowed the first mouthful of Spanish chicken I knew what that meant: we were having take-away McDonald's that Friday. On the 12th of June I posted a picture on social media of me accomplishing my goal. By then everyone who was following my recovery knew from Sam's updates that this had been a long-term goal of mine, but I had a touch of sadness when I thought of the person responsible for setting it – Politeness from Lewisham. I had no way of contacting her and she would never know or have that job satisfaction that should be hers. Sam had to chop it up so I could eat it with a fork. It took me half an hour to consume the Big Mac and it was cold by the end but to me it tasted of prayers, therapy, love, and hard work.

After that experience we re-established our family tradition of having a Friday night takeaway together. My weight had dropped three stone since the strokes but over the next few months it increased a whole stone such was the variety of food I was now enjoying. The staff got wind of our tradition and would always jealously ask me every Friday "What takeaway are you having tonight?" I think I was responsible for increased takeaway sales in Southwest London during that time.

Poo Bum Wee

The bladder being a muscle sack meant mine needed to recover strength and control from its paralysis as well. I was still wearing adult nappies on weekdays and going to the loo a lot. A young consultant took it upon himself to talk to me about it and politely give me some tips on bladder control. After he'd finished I just looked at him and said, "If I'm still having problems in a year you've got a point, but for now I really don't care because I'm alive." He looked at me and smiled "Fair enough."

I still needed assistance to do a 'No.2' and on one weekend at home my greatest fear came true – Sam had to wipe my bottom. We'd jokingly promised each other we'd do that if we were elderly and infirm but neither of us expected that to be at the age of forty-eight. Utter humiliation for me but I couldn't help thinking were there no depths to which Sam wouldn't stoop (metaphorically *and* literally). It became my new goal to be able to wipe my own bottom but to spare mine and my room mates blushes I thought those exercises would be best kept for night-time.

A Cat Needs a Cat Flap

There were changes at Putney and at home at that time. Big Money went home consigned to a life in a wheelchair because neuroplasticity never did reconnect his left side. Meanwhile a Muslim Italian man who spoke no English took up the spare bed in our room. The same day I saw him mysteriously try to walk out of his wheelchair by himself and fall over, breaking his arm. As he was rushed to Accident and Emergency I was glad the physios at Lewisham had not let me try to stand when I was not ready for it.

I eventually did my presentation about my recovery to staff, explaining what it's like communicating whilst locked-in with a demonstration between myself and Giggle, and sharing the role I believed my faith was playing in my recovery. It was gratifying to see my consultant writing notes because whatever she thought about my faiths' involvement I was now a medical fact sitting there in front of her.

I had to go back to St George's hospital for a bubble echo scan on my heart. They were still trying to find out why I'd had the strokes, but that drew a blank as they found no holes in my heart. As we pulled up in the hospital transfer ambulance I looked at the building 'So this is where I was in intensive care' I pondered. I felt divine closeness in my heart – He had been here that day and had whispered in my heart. As I was wheeled in the main entrance we passed the café Sam had said she'd spent that first week crying in. Instead of feeling sad about that visualisation I felt victorious to be overcoming the hopeless chances of survival the consultant had given Sam. It was beginning to hold a special place in my heart.

Weekends were becoming much easier for me now. The physios were letting the carers help transfer me in and out of the car on Friday nights and Monday mornings. My sit-ups and my leg exercises were clearly working as Samuel didn't need to support me getting into the car anymore and I could just about drag my left leg up into the car by itself. I also got a chance to let Beamer sit in 'Black Shadow' and see what it was like. "Very nice Mr David, I'll buy it!" he laughed.

"You should write a book" was becoming a common line carers were saying to me because of all the progress I was making. They had no idea that the Lewisham nurses had said the same thing, so at weekends I started typing notes with one hand for this book. I started keeping records of my own about my recovery because Sam's notes were tailing off, but I got a bit carried away and even mentioned about putting a cat flap in for our promised cat and about Beamer and In Charge always wanting house renovation photos.

Being home at weekends brought plenty of time to reflect together on what had happened to us, usually provoked by innocuous things like seeing all my recorded programmes waiting to be watched from the 3rd of November. But one memorable dark time sticks in my mind. On the late May bank holiday weekend I had a meltdown. The constant pain in my joints, the unexplained sensations all over my skin, the discomfort of my face, the unending tiredness I was still experiencing, my vision and balance problems, the exhaustion of pushing myself to constantly exercise – it all got on top of me. I was wrestling with how long I'd have to suffer to be 'okay.' "If this is what I have to go through to fulfil my purpose in life I'm not sure I want it!" I screamed and spluttered between breaths. Sam could tell I was in turmoil about it and I could see she felt powerless. When I'd calmed down and the muscle spasms and choking had receded we decided to go out for a drive and reflected a bit by visiting some of our old haunts – it was just the tonic. 'I don't think many in history have cruised into their life's purpose' I reasoned, as I stared through the windscreen.

Electrocution!

Sessions were now in full swing in the Covid-free environment of Putney and Tunes was back at her keyboard with me warbling along. Our socially distanced music group started up again and I was back on form, stealing Sophie's playlist for song choices.

Occupational therapy started up gradually and Task Master knew that time was running out before I was due to leave. So she cleverly upped the ante on my stubborn claw left hand by using Functional Electrical Stimulation (FES) or as I call it - 'electrocution.' After sessions had finished she'd stick pads on my forearm for thirty minutes in certain positions which connected via cables to a control unit she held. At first it seemed like an implement of torture because we had to work out the right power level to put through it to get the desired effect. Let's just say it was a shocking experience the first few times. The electrical pulses then acted to enhance my brain signals to open my hand which felt wonderful after eight months of a clenched fist. It was a way for me to be able to exercise my weak back hand tendons. I could tell this was going to be another long journey back from paralysis.

Cobbler also used electrocution on my left ankle which temporarily took away the jelly feeling in my ankle and really helped my footing when we did sessions walking hand-in-hand. She also tried it once on my weak left butt cheek. It didn't work but was comical.

My shorts were round my ankles as I stood leaning on the plinth in front of me. My nappy was pulled back exposing my butt cheek with the pads stuck to it. Cobbler and a female assistant were staring intently at my bottom. We were all giggling which caused another female physio assistant to peer behind the privacy screens requesting "Can I have a look? I've never seen FES in use before." She started giggling too. Then The Gaffer worked out what was going on and he started hurling friendly insults "What are you doing in there with those young ladies Mr Hazeldine? Remember you're a married vicar!" Honestly, you couldn't make it up.

Time was moving on and having weekend leave was helping me stay fresh for my fight back from paralysis but it wasn't lost on me that we were getting closer to my discharge date of Friday the 3rd of July. Without using electrocution on my left ankle I wasn't remotely near my goal of walking freehand again. I needed something to happen…

Sixteen

Getting Ready to Go Home

The summer months started well with Cobbler getting me a two-handed wheelchair. It was tough to control and slow to wheel at first because of the disparity between the strength of both my arms. I was just glad Task Master's work on my left side was starting to pay off in a very practical way though. I caused many corridor traffic jams and often said to the therapists as they collected me for their session "You'd better push me or we'll be here all day."

Why She Loved Me

I was beyond the need for a transfer aid of any kind by now which was a momentous result for my exercising. My left leg would still vibrate, buckle and sway awkwardly under my own weight but a carers hand steadied me as I learned to take two sideways steps in a transfer. It felt marvellously normal to be free of transfer aids now and motivated me to do one-legged standing practise at weekends in the Rotunda to make this experience safer.

Surprisingly learning to step-turn would bring me the most significant moment in our marriage. It was a Friday night and we'd just got home from 'work,' and I needed a No.2. The builders had constructed the new side extension loo to a usable state and we had to use it whilst they took out the old family bathroom. It was a squeeze because it was only designed for one person.

I stood up with no transfer aid, holding onto the sink whilst Sam squeezed behind to wipe my bottom. Then it happened. After she and I had washed our hands we found each other looking eye to eye with no transfer aid in the way. We were both caught unawares by the moment but immediately hugged without a second thought. It was automatic after nine months of physical separation. Tears streamed down our faces as she held me tight and I reciprocated with my right arm. Such was the depth of feeling that neither of us could get any words out for crying and we definitely didn't need an alphabet board to help – we just knew.

A thousand thoughts flooded my mind: Sam holding my hand as if holding onto my life in intensive care, her kissing my paralysed lips every day on arrival in Lewisham, me feeling overwhelmed with her devotion, her crying into my bed sheets as she began to accept that something marvellous was happening with my recovery, her comforting hand when I told her of my suicidal thoughts, our first moment standing eye-to-eye during my physio session whilst on the Cyra Steady, the desperation she'd felt when separated by lockdown, the torment she must have experienced when I contracted Covid - but now here we were finally in each other's arms again. In that moment we were okay.

Since our marriage I've always wondered why Sam loved me. I could be snappy, proud, angry, argumentative, insensitive without realising it and plenty more besides. Yes I could be funny, adventurous, driven and (dare I say) was handsome to her, but those changeable characteristics are not enough to marry someone, follow them around in their spiritual calling, produce two kids, live in perpetual building sites, and enjoy twenty-seven close years together. But in that hug I realised why she loved me - because she was loving. When she said her wedding vows she meant them not because of who I was but because of who she was. She had decided to set her affections on me and that was that. Had I been experiencing divine love through her all these years and not realised it? Probably.

Divine Irony

Just before Covid hit and he was discharged I'd seen Bus Driver walking up and down the gym in a white frame on wheels. He rested his elbows on its pads to help carry his weight and grasped its vertical handles. It was inspiring but a stage too far for me back then, so you can imagine my excitement when Cobbler wanted me to try the same frame even with my cast on.

She raised her eyebrows at me when she said, "It's called a pulpit frame." Oh, the irony. I first tried it during a physio session with her around the ward with The Gaffer assisting from behind. I would often accidently lean too much on it and would feel it getting away from me, so I'd have to jerk it back and correct my stance. I felt my goal of walking was in jeopardy because time was ticking down to my discharge and I didn't feel I was looking good for progression beyond it.

The physios would leave the pulpit frame opposite me at nights in the empty bay recently vacated by Cranky. It would almost cry out to me at night inspiring me to keep exercising and engaging with physio sessions even though I wasn't sure how I was going to progress from that. I was sure I'd stand behind a real pulpit and preach again one day.

The 14th of May was a watershed moment: I did my first update on Facebook. Ever since the first week back in November Sam had been giving updates on my recovery but now my friends and followers could hear directly from me. They were astounded to hear from me by my own hand and it was just wonderful to be able to reply to each individual response, making my own personal contact with people in the outside world. I had just been getting on with my recovery so was surprised by how inspired people had been by it. The update showed me walking with Cobbler holding only my hand. I felt like Wobbly and my own personal English Channel in my head didn't help.

With a month and a half left The Gaffer and other physio assistants got me walking holding their hand as much as possible – to the shower, around the ward, and in sessions. One time we did the whole length of the gym and back again to where a group of physios were standing in a circle having a chat. We joined them and I let go of The Gaffer's hand and joined in the conversation with no-one batting an eyelid. I was managing to hold it benefitting from my weekend standing but Tour Guide noticed after a few minutes saying, "Sorry David, I didn't think, let's get you a chair." I must have looked slightly normal.

In the years to come I could realistically imagine Sam and I walking hand in hand along the Thames towpath. But to get to that point I needed more specific work on my hamstring and Cobbler, still 'making it up as she went along,' had an ingenious idea.

She suggested using a skateboard for hamstring retractions and with gritted teeth I managed one retraction of a few centimetres on a hard floor. It had been a long journey to this point with my 'beat the hamstring' exercise each night and now it was going to be another long journey using this to get to the point where I could do proper hamstring curls laying on my front. I was straight on a video chat afterwards asking Sam to order one online.

A few days later a bright luminous orange skateboard arrived for me at Putney. Beamer took full advantage "Look at me, Mr David!" he would exclaim like a child as he wheeled across my room between the beds. I used it loads each day along with wheeling round the ward in my two-handed wheelchair, OT arm exercises, Therabite, daytime sessions and night-time exercises - I basically didn't stop moving. Every muscle in my body needed to be stronger to give me any hope of free walking and the jeopardy of missing my goal propelled me on.

As Cool as an Old Lady

Shouty was using a Zimmer frame so naturally I wanted to transition from the pulpit frame to that. I didn't think I was as steady as I needed to be on the pulpit frame to transition to one, but I kept asking Cobbler if I could try it to find out. But a month before I was due to leave she gave me some bad news. "We've had a Zimmer frame on order for the last few weeks for you but it hasn't come yet." 'The pandemic' I thought. Was that going to try and hinder my recovery again? "But we do have a walker you could try" she said. "Why don't you see if you can get over to the desk with it?" She presented me with an old ladies walker with four legs, wheels, and a basket – presumably for shopping at M&S. 'Oh well,' I thought, 'my dignity's already gone.'

I slowly edged my way over to the desk. My left hand was so weak it couldn't hold the handle properly but my thumb was wedged in place keeping it gripping. I still had my casting on my left foot, so I didn't feel in danger of my foot flipping over. I used the handlebar break under my right hand if I felt it running away from me. The main thing I noticed though was that most people were smaller than me again like normal. If this were ever to be my mode of transport there would be no more looking up at people, no more chins, no more ceilings but my usual view of the crown of people's heads – how I'd missed it.

When I got to the desk I felt okay so for a laugh I walked towards the gym's star trek exit expecting Cobbler to call me back. Instead she just said "Okay, we're going out the door are we?" When I got outside I could see the door leading to the lift was stuck open and thought 'That's only about ten metres - I can do that.' Once through the door the lift was right there 'That'll be a challenge' I thought. One thing led to another and I ended up doing a one hundred metre walk to just outside my room. It would have been cool to walk in but my legs were vibrating which was the sign I needed to slump back into my wheelchair that Cobbler was wheeling behind me. "Well done, David. I'd say that's your first independent walk!" I looked at her in a bit of shock when she used the word 'independent.' "What about the Zimmer frame?" I asked. "Evidently you don't need it." I was steadier than I thought.

Several things just tumbled away as I started using the walker on the ward. I would never step-turn again, meaning transfers to and from the car at weekends were much easier, I could go to the loo by myself whenever I wanted so I'd never wet myself again, Sam never had to wipe my bottom again because I was forced to practise it myself to maintain independence, and I could use the walker myself to get to the shower.

Needless to say walking round the ward became another daily exercise. Vertigo and fears of falling backwards undermined my confidence but mind control and deep breathing helped me overcome my hesitancy. I had worked so hard to get here I wasn't going to let fear rob me of my newfound independence. I looked laboured, jolty, and was painfully slow but I knew my trajectory was only going one way.

Accolade

Late in June we got the wonderful news Sam and I had been hoping for. Task Master obtained external NHS funding for me to stay on a final six weeks from the 3rd of July until Friday the 14th of August – it was like an accolade for everyone involved in my recovery. Though we both missed each other so much during the week we knew it was the right decision to accept the extension. "We think we can get you home without the need for daily carers" said Task Master. My goal of free walking had just got a massive boost.

From that moment on everything changed. Occupational therapy and physio sessions were no longer about individual limbs and trying to walk but were about living independently at home in my current disabled state. Preparing a basic meal, using the walker outside on uneven surfaces, using steps, getting up and dressing myself, even showering myself. I can still remember overhearing the surprised carers voices outside the shower room one morning when they asked Task Master, "Where's David?" "He's inside showering alone." "Alone, ooh!"

I refocused my exercises with nurse Sam's help too. We developed new rolling exercises to help me get out of bed myself and more left leg specific exercises. It sounded like a dream at the moment but we agreed that if we were to sleep together after my discharge I should get used to doing my exercises first thing in the morning and not during the night. I started doing left leg standing at work every day too, tightly holding my bed bars, and I was now doing sit ups with my whole back just lifting off the mattress.

Twice in those final six weeks my body conked out. I'd been thrashing it morning, noon, and night for the last six months and it was protesting. It wasn't a question of lack of will-power it just wouldn't respond. All around me staff were taking annual leave and it made me realise my body needed some too. I rested from exercising on both those days and just completed my usual rehab sessions slowly. I decided I'd have a week's rest after discharge.

It wasn't only my sessions and exercises that changed but room compositions changed too. The bed opposite me was filled by The Math Lad. He still had his vacant look and droopy head which I'd found unnerving at first but now I knew his story I didn't feel that way anymore. I was one of many cheering him on as he began to softly whisper his first words in two years. Other patients arrived and they had their names written up on the board in the Day Room to be signed in and out of therapy sessions. When I arrived at Putney back in January all our names were printed out on magnetic strips but since Covid that had stopped. Now only two magnetic strips remained, me and Shouty. He'd arrived just before Covid, so by virtue of my progress I'd become the longest serving patient.

Family Hug

It was Sam's birthday and Sophie had finished university. Along with Samuel all three of them came to collect me that Friday afternoon. It was the first time we were all back together since the hospital lockdown started back in March. I stood out of my chair in the car park and gave Sophie an emotional one-armed hug. "Dad! You've really progressed" she exclaimed. However, the best hug was saved for home.

Since the kids were young we've always had family hugs. Initially Sophie between us with Samuel in his nappy on Sam's hip. Then years later Samuel would be standing and Sam and I would bend down to be closer to their heads, then the kids grew to be under our chins and now after the strokes Samuel had shot up and was almost as tall as me. I stood in the Rotunda and the family crowded round. As we felt each other's arms around our backs once again we kissed and cried with happiness – our family bond not devasted.

I was so thankful for all Sam was, for what she'd carried this past year, and for what she was doing with the house. Sophie bought me a birthday card I could hand sign messily for her but I knew my lability would spoil the moment preventing me from getting my words out, so I wrote an email expressing love and appreciation for her. She cried reading it saying, "That's the best email ever."

By now the new kitchen was in and the flooring down, the dining room table and chairs were in and 'Big Sis' provided us with a temporary settee before all our possessions came from Belvedere later that month. The rest of the house was being decorated now with fresh paint fumes replacing the tired, old, dusty odours of the previous occupant.

It was a lovely, hot, July Sunday afternoon that weekend and our bi-fold doors were wide open so we could enjoy the garden view. Sam rested her head on my shoulder as we sat on the temporary sofa just as she had that Christmas Eve night back in our youth when I first asked her out. It was the first time since the strokes I'd sat on anything other than a hospital bed, plinth, or wheelchair. Tears welled up in our eyes as we listened to a contemporary Christian worship song about seeing victories out of darkness because you 'know how this story ends.' I don't think the writer had knowing you were going to survive locked-in syndrome in mind when they wrote it but it was a special moment all the same. The emotion of the last nine months was coming out and our hearts were full of thankfulness and relief for how things were turning out. "Remind me not to wear mascara at weekends again" blubbed Sam.

The Epitomes

The calendar was saying I had just over two weeks left now and one midweek afternoon I was organising my phone for my new life in Surrey. It prompted me to text the social worker I had seen in Lewisham about the alcoholic we'd been helping together and about my neighbour Mr Belvedere from Lewisham. He replied almost immediately with updates: both were now firmly ensconced in nursing homes. The alcoholic I was glad for because he couldn't look after himself but I was surprised by Mr Belvedere's final destination. He had been physically so far ahead of me so it hit home again like a tonne of bricks: my recovery was rare and was the epitome of mercy.

It's true that I was having a remarkable recovery, it's true that it was drawing praise from therapists, and it's true my case was interesting consultants, but it was also true there was another side to my recovery. In the interests of integrity I shared this in a social media post. There had been pain, defeat, failure, suicidal thoughts, and isolation; there were irritating sensations on parts of my skin, my face still felt heavy, my left foot was still a problem, my left hand and arm were pretty much useless, my balance was shot and my eyesight was weird.

I was also to become acquainted with PTSD (Post Traumatic Stress Disorder). It first came on slowly one afternoon then twice more triggered by events. For me it was characterised by racing thoughts of the devastation I'd experienced and what could have been, and by panting breath and uncontrollable emotions for about fifteen minutes.

The worst episode was when The Math Lad moved on to long term care and I was told a patient with a trachea was moving in. I couldn't understand why this had been allowed to happen opposite me but was told he was not responding to therapy and was waiting for a nursing home, so his private room was needed. I wheeled myself out of my room and down to the end of the corridor, just sitting there with my mind racing.

I discovered mind control during my recovery which is a wonderful thing. Sitting there I reasoned that this could keep on happening and I could be triggered by all kinds of things: What if I happened to see a stroke awareness advert on the television? What if I were watching a game show and the host says to the contender "I need to lock in your answer…"? What if I hear a noise resembling a suction machine – like on a house renovation site? I had to face it, think through my possible reactions and think of coping strategies.

I slowly wheeled myself back to my room to be confronted with my new neighbour opposite me. I was ready for any triggers that might induce PTSD but not for what I saw. He was the epitome of what Musical Gangster had described to me when showering me back in my first week – someone who had given up. Over my last few weeks I would have to watch this man, who was my age and bizarrely had a similar sounding name to me, listen to heartbreak love songs out loud from dawn till dusk. He was fed by carers but could move his hands and control his iPad. Therapists constantly cajoled him to take part in rehab but he hadn't been willing for months. He was pining for a life lost and didn't want to do anything.

As harsh as it may sound for me to say this but he didn't need to do anything for himself either. He was washed, changed, and fed by others; his every need attended to. Medically, he was in the best place possible and his destination, a nursing home, would have costs covered by the state as he had no savings or property (confirmed in a phone call I overheard with a friend) – everything was done for him. I know what it is to be that low and I understand brain injury symptoms are usually overwhelming. But it's not over till it's over. I was sad for him but thankful that I was not of that ilk and grateful too for people's prayers, Sam and my family and the therapists who kept me going on my fight back from paralysis.

Finishing the Road

It happened on Friday the 10th of July just before lunch – I finally walked freehand. "David, you're going to have to take some risks if you want to walk" Cobbler kept saying. The risk was falling but the reward was walking. By nature I'm a calculated risk-taker. To be involved in property development you are always calculating the risks of losing your financial investment against the reward of getting a return on that investment. Usually you have to say "No" to investment opportunities many times but say "Yes" once. And there was one thing stopping me from saying "Yes" to taking the risk of walking.

My left foot and heel would have to feel sturdier somehow before I'd have a go. The previous week I'd walked freehand when my right leg was down, but had used Cobblers' hand for my left footstep, so I knew I was close. But the air cast I permanently wore around my left ankle now wasn't enough for me to take the risk and try free walking. "Let me try something…" said Cobbler as she dashed away to her drawer.

She pulled out an old casting of mine she'd kept, cut the front part away so I could get my leg in it, then wiggled it on my foot. "Try that." I stood holding her hand and noticed how firm my left ankle felt. I sat down and thought about it, looked up at her and said, "Let's take a risk." I stood and took two short pigeon steps freehand with Cobbler by my side. She pulled my wheelchair close again and I sat down. Tears streamed down my face as I convulsed uncontrollably with joy and relief whilst she ran and got some tissues. "It's perfectly normal David, you just walked again!"

After I'd composed myself, we agreed to do it properly. I was to walk freehand across the gym to the opposite plinth. It was the culmination of everything I'd been aiming for all along. All I was thinking was 'Don't get excited but… I'm walking!' My walk wasn't pretty mind, and it took a lot of concentration. I had stuttering steps due to my left leg still being like a plank of wood, my left hip sagged, my whole body felt like a tonne of bricks, my lability made me sob and wobble, tears made it hard to see properly, and my head felt like the English Channel causing imbalance – but I made it.

I sat in my wheelchair eating lunch dazed at what had just transpired. Emotions were rushing through me. I didn't have any afternoon sessions, so I had time to watch the video back, speak with Sam, message my family, bask in the fact that faith had now become a reality and enjoy thoughts of what "You're going to be okay" was now looking like. I had purpose coursing through my veins imagining myself walking to a pulpit to tell my story and I was bubbling with excitement to see the family in a few hours – it was a joyous reunion that afternoon to say the least.

I still needed my raised heel and foot inversion to be addressed to make it safer to walk without carers. Fortunately, Cobbler had foreseen this and made an appointment to get me moulded for a bespoke cast months before but due to Covid so many appointments were being put back. I was disappointed by this inevitability hanging over me knowing it would probably jeopardise my free walking for months.

Astonishingly though, my appointment for casting came through normally for two weeks before discharge and it would be ready for collection in time. They also put me on a long waiting list for an operation where I could have my left heel dropped down and my inversion corrected to give me a flat foot to walk on, thus eventually doing away with the need for the cast altogether. I didn't even know they could do that kind of thing. But for now with a custom cast giving me enough stability to walk a few steps, I had only one thing on my mind.

Walking Out of Hospital

After three extensions to my discharge date and Covid delays, the day for my departure finally arrived – Friday the 14th of August 2020. The week leading up to it had been peppered with carers who would not be on shift that day saying their personal 'goodbyes.' Top-Notch

Temp even woke me up at 10pm to say her 'goodbyes' congratulating me on a recovery that had so inspired her.

My last session before lunch was speech and language in which Giggle did such an encouraging thing. She knew I needed muscle strength for continued recovery at home, so with her church background she pulled together Bible verses all about God giving people strength. Unbeknownst to her they were exactly the ones Mum put on my wall in Lewisham. We used them in the session for pronunciation practice.

I sat in the Day Room that afternoon with a large chocolate cake that Sam had got me. It was to say 'Thanks' to all the staff who'd become like a temporary family. I'd sent an email to several therapists and staff earlier in the week to say a detailed 'Thank you.' I was aware emotional lability could spoil the occasion if I tried to say what I really felt. The email subject title read, 'When 'thanks' is not enough.'

On a day shift for once, Jolly Dancer had kindly packed all my belongings which waited on a trolley for my 4pm departure. As carers and therapists passed by, the cake gradually disappeared, Tunes and Musical Gangster among them. Even the chirpy physio who'd played cards with me during Covid popped in from another ward.

The time had come for me to leave rehab the way I had wanted to all along. Cobbler wheeled me to the Drapers Ward electronic double doors and stood holding them open. A small crowd gathered behind me clapping and cheering as I stood up out of my wheelchair and walked out into the corridor. I'd rehearsed this moment over and over in my mind for months and personally it lived up to its billing.

Not making a very good effort to control my emotional lability my mind was flooded with thoughts: I'd arrived through these doors locked-in, paralysed, on oxygen, with a trachea, and now to be walking out of them eight months later felt like the apex of mercy; the darkness of suicidal thoughts versus the elation when my left big toe moved; my promise to Stu that I'd WORK SO HARD IN PUTNEY had been fulfilled every night as I flopped exhaustedly into bed; my therapists' and family's continued support even in the face of Covid, and Sam's unfailing devotion spurring me on.

I sat back down in my wheelchair to be wheeled down the very long, high corridors to my waiting family. All my therapists and a bunch of carers followed behind. They started up the clapping and cheering again as Sam and I embraced in the car park. Even the chaplain who I hadn't seen since lockdown just 'happened' to be walking past and said a quick prayer with us both.

Just before we drove home for the final time Sam did something that previously would have been totally out of character for a lady who hated public speaking. She was very comfortable just watching her husband address crowds of people all his life but now Sam turned the tables and spontaneously addressed the crowd herself. Her profuse thankfulness had got the better of her. I was in 'Black Shadow' by this time and was looking on totally surprised.

Sam, of course, had been affected by the events of the last ten months, so doing something like that was like water off a ducks back now. She will tell you in her own words what the last ten months were like from her perspective…

Seventeen
I Didn't Get That Memo

Right before my eyes, just like one of those horrible television stroke adverts, 'it' happened. David lost consciousness, collapsing backwards into a wheelchair brought up behind him by the paramedic, threw up and the whole right side of his face dropped. Everything after that was a blur.

The alarm suddenly sounded and within seconds he was surrounded by numerous shouting medical staff lifting him onto a trolley. A sense of panic dramatically filled the room. They sliced his top off from waist to neck exposing his bare chest and doctors started working on him. He was fitting and spitting and he kept trying to tell us about his jaw clenching together. I had been pushed to one side by now, so I just kept shouting "Is he having a stroke?" "What's happening?" and "Is he going to be okay?!" No-one was answering my remonstrations as they all focussed on David's survival. I thrive on organisation and planning but in this moment I was ruthlessly stripped of all control and felt utterly helpless. I do remember a blonde-haired nurse tutting and complaining as David accidentally spat on her whilst fitting. I kept apologising to her "He's not like this... this isn't normal... he's never angry like this... he's a vicar."

A doctor told me they were taking him immediately for a brain scan. That would take fifteen minutes, so a lovely nurse sat me down and offered me a cup of tea. I wasn't given much information at this stage because it was too early to know but a doctor soon explained David had a large blood clot from a stroke that needed treatment. He would need clot busting drugs which

Woolwich Hospital couldn't offer so he was to be transferred immediately under blue flashing lights to The Princess Royal University Hospital, Orpington. I didn't go in the ambulance with him as I needed to take our car in case we had to go elsewhere.

Tubes Everywhere

The sat nav guided me across London that night giving me the opportunity to call all the family hands-free and let them know what was happening. But I mainly spoke with my sister for comfort and to make plans, every so often interspersing the conversation with repetitive "What's just happened?" "Is he going to be okay?"

A consultant at Orpington confirmed David had a blood clot in his brain and administered the drugs to help dissipate it. He explained a surgeon at St George's, Tooting, was also available to try and urgently remove it. By now David's parents had managed to join me from Surrey. At a moment's notice even at this late hour they'd whizzed round the southern M25 and found me.

Their help meant I could drop off our car at home on the way to St George's, quickly get a few clothes and my laptop and jump into their car. They had set up a pillow in the back seat so I could try and get some rest but my racing mind meant my eyes were not willing to close.

The operation was unsuccessful because the blood clot was located in the pons area of the brain stem, so they would need to keep David sedated for the next 24 hours to see if the drugs alone would dissipate the clot. Confused and still wanting to know what had happened to David we were just told to go home and rest as there was nothing else that could be done – it was just a matter of waiting.

Climbing into David's teenage bed at his parent's house I was exhausted mentally and physically. I felt numb and alone. Trying to get some sleep was a waste of time. If I did manage to drift off I'd wake up soon after remembering everything that had happened and that David was lying in the Neuroscience Intensive Care Unit by himself, his life hanging by a thread. It was simply awful and I couldn't stop crying. I was counting down the hours for when my sister would get here with Samuel from his sleepover and Sophie from university, so we could all be together and see Daddy at the hospital first thing in the morning.

I apprehensively went into David's bay that first morning by myself. Not knowing what to expect I was confronted with an image I would prefer to forget. David was sedated and oblivious to his precarious situation. He had tubes all over going into his body doing things I still don't know about. With his life support machine beside him and twenty-four-hour one-to-one nurse care he was being kept alive. Just yesterday he was complaining of a persistent headache while watching motor racing – and now this.

I found myself facing an awful decision: do I let the kids see him like this? It could be their last memory and I didn't want that for them but I knew I couldn't keep them from him because it might be their last time to speak to him and say 'goodbye.' I felt so alone making that decision. My parenting had been about trying to protect my children and this was something I just couldn't protect them from. It was happening. I knew they had to have the opportunity to talk to him despite not knowing if he could even hear them. We all sobbed together at his bedside speaking loving words and breathing out our sorrows in prayer.

Ten Percent

The early days involved many family meetings with the consultant. I was told a lot of things that first week, so I had to write them down because my head was so frazzled. The upshot of it was that he had had a devastating brain stem ischaemic stroke of the pons area along with three other smaller strokes. In one particular meeting I remember the female consultant saying that if David had only had the three other strokes we wouldn't be needing to have 'this' conversation. It was little comfort because we were going to have 'that chat.'

She told me his type of brain stem stroke was extremely rare. The brain stem controls the breathing, consciousness, all limbs and nearly every other internal organ. Because they couldn't remove the blood clot she gave David only a ten to twenty percent chance of survival. If he were to survive, he would remain on life support for the rest of his life living in an institution requiring round the clock medical care. She proceeded to tell me how sorry she was and that this extremely rare type of brain stem stroke was so cruel; it might leave him aware that he was paralysed and trapped inside his own body called 'locked-in' syndrome. I thought 'It would feel crueller if he died' – nothing was making sense. But little did I know that everything was making sense to David after hearing The Voice tell him he'd be okay – I most certainly didn't get that memo. My journey into faith throughout that crisis was somewhat more gradual.

By Monday they started reducing David's sedation so they could try to communicate with him and try to establish the extent of his brain damage. Two speech and language female therapists came out from communicating with David through an alphabet board asking if the words 'Lewis' and 'car' meant anything? My first reaction was panic 'It's all on me to ascertain what David is trying to communicate' because I know him better than anyone. I failed miserably. All I could think of was 'Why is David asking about a friend's car we've not seen for a few years?' I started to wonder 'Or is he referring to 'Black Shadow' we'd just bought?'

and 'Was he all there?' With little clarity they went back in to try again.

My relief was huge when they came out having established David was asking if Lewis Hamilton had become F1 World Champion after the grand prix race that weekend. Elation broke out among the gathered family. It meant David remembered the very last thing he was watching on television, it meant he had a concept of time, it also meant he was all there and that we all had a way to communicate with him.

Survival Mode

The many hours I spent each day by David's bedside were mainly me comforting him with updates of where he was, what was happening and what had happened. I didn't know if his brain could retain everything, so I was quite repetitive. His body was incredibly tired and just the act of blinking at letters on the alphabet board was too much after a few minutes.

Having established that his faith was still intact I thought it would be good to ask him what Bible verse he might like me to read him. It took me four days to work out which book of the Bible he wanted me to read to him but it was worth it because the passage he chose was not for his benefit but mine. Very quickly after that I became a master of the alphabet board and was taking every opportunity to show all the nurses how best to communicate with him because I knew I couldn't be by his side twenty-four hours a day. This was his voice to the outside world after all but sadly none of them took it on for some reason.

We were all in survival mode initially. It wasn't a matter of planning anything or thinking ahead rather just living hour by hour. Everyone on both sides of the family rallied round and established fantastic support to facilitate the children and I being able to see David as much as possible. Rotas had to be set up for family visiting because it was tightly restricted, only ignored once for our longstanding friends Clive and Jane to anoint David with oil for healing.

The power of social media was hugely helpful as I became David's voice on his Facebook page. My updates and prayer requests were commonly met with shock at the severity and suddenness of all this. Many had to re-read them a few times to help take it in. Very soon it became overwhelming trying to juggle reaching out to people whilst spending time with David and I had to stop. People would understand I needed to be there for David and him alone. My boss was hugely supportive and enabled me to take time off to give much needed devotion to David.

In hindsight I think the stress and trauma of what had happened had kicked in and I was simply trying to get through each day as best I could. I spent many a moment driving to and from the hospital bursting into tears and trying to pull myself together to avoid crashing. One time in that first week I visited David from my sister's home in Surrey by train with my brother-in-law. He was a regular commuter to London and would accompany me because I was in no fit state to negotiate the journey alone. I fell asleep on his shoulder on the tube dribbling on his suit jacket with tears running down my face. For once not caring what people thought, I was just trying to keep myself together. He walked me right to the hospital door because I couldn't navigate the route and I left him there not even saying goodbye – I was just lost in a world of swirling nightmares.

The hospital café was my go-to place for breaks and the people there respected my privacy, letting me quietly sob into my coffee and be alone with my thoughts. I just didn't know if David was going to pull through because to make things worse (if they could get any worse) he contracted a chest infection that could kill him in his weakened state.

I wondered what our family life would look like if he did pull through. I felt powerless to protect our children from how our lives were inevitably going to change by what their dad might become. David was always the strong and capable one in our relationship, giving guidance and loving leadership, helping us all navigate life and find the best in everything. It seemed that all that had gone and I was now the one having to carry everything on my shoulders. I tried not to focus too much on what the future might hold; him never coming home, severe disability for the rest of his life, the medical support required and how he could still be a father to our children in that state. Our world and all we knew of it had been devastated.

My faith deepened in those days, drawing strength from the Lord because I had no inner strength – I felt truly broken hearted. I found deep comfort in a Bible verse I came across in the Psalms reassuring me that 'The Lord is close to the broken hearted.' Also knowing a multitude of prayers were going up for us, it's hard to put down in writing but I just felt 'carried.'

Unbelievably they had to move David from St George's to our local stroke specialist hospital in Lewisham because of budgets. Assured by them that it was a common thing, it nonetheless gave me more stress. Then on admittance I had to painfully relive everything in detail to the new consultant in case anything important was missing in his notes. To my anger he categorised David as DNR (Do Not Resuscitate) if he had a cardiac arrest despite my pleas that David and I would always choose life no matter what that looked like. I was told it was not mine or David's decision to take but rather was the medical teams because David's health was so weak and critical he would not survive if he were to suffer one.

The consultant took me into a private room and asked me how I was doing. I burst into tears as I poured out my thoughts and feelings. I then had to listen to him tell me that though the swelling on David's brain had reduced, I still needed to prepare myself and the children for the worst. Apparently it was highly likely that he would go on to have a further stroke in the next few weeks or months.

Game Changer

You can imagine the emotional rollercoaster I was on. From that first bleak week in St George's to the current high of being told that David had come off life support on his first day in Lewisham; him not having to be institutionalised and having the hope that coming home instead might now be possible; it was sheer elation when I was told his chest infection was under control. The children and I had many tears of relief because these were all game changers. The feeling of vulnerability was receding and we were entering a new phase of stabilisation.

Throughout his two months' stay in Lewisham David received wonderful care by the nurses and I was embraced by all the therapists in their work on him. They were long days for me and I would spend many hours by David's bedside every day for both our sakes with family regularly coming to visit him too. Having spent each day communicating with David through the alphabet board, I hated leaving each evening. I was often crying down the ward corridor out of David's sight but the nurses always saw.

Journeys to and from the hospital each day were nerve-racking because I was mindful everything was on me now, so I needed to keep safe and stay well. I was updating everyone through social media again, ensuring the children were cared for and looked after, managing visitors, supporting David every day and everything else that comes with running a family home, not to mention David communicating the immediate need to BUY A HOUSE amid all that.

A New Greeting

It was a very long two months. I still had in the back of my mind what the St George's and Lewisham consultants had told me about preparing for the worst but yet each day we were beginning to see small signs of hope.

After a while David started to greet me most mornings through the alphabet board with 'Don't get excited but ...' and then he would proceed to communicate which part of his body had started gingerly moving overnight. The excitement over early flickers in his right fingers and perfect movement restored in his right ankle fuelled my hope for a chance of recovery. The morning when I was greeted with a verbal 'Hello Sam' just enhanced this.

Amongst those many good days there were a few where he just didn't want to communicate because he was too tired or was thinking about things. I found those days hardest when the children were visiting. Once he communicated to me with the children looking on WILL I BE A VEGETABLE I was so cross with him for asking that in front of them and confused by his selfishness for asking but I've since found out this communication was a mistake and he meant ARE THEY SAYING ILL BE A VEGETABLE It was so hard juggling support for David in moments like these whilst also supporting the children and coming to terms with everything myself as well. But through it all David never once gave in to anger or resentment from becoming severely disabled so suddenly.

Tis the Season to Be Jolly

I'm a busy person by nature and my capacity has always been high but even I had to operate on a whole new emotional level. Christmas was coming up presenting logistical nightmares about how we'd still celebrate it whilst trying to lift the spirits of our children. At the same time I was having to be entirely practical and sort out Samuel's current and future education and do the new house search.

I learned to lean on our family's ready support during those days. My sister Sharon was a rock, enabled by my wonderful brother-in-law Dom, who dropped everything to support me and the children throughout. Stuart researched and investigated rehabilitation options; Mark set up and organised the group family chat so they could arrange regular visiting themselves and the kids handled the decorations. On Christmas Day itself Sue and Paul provided our traditional Christmas games around David's bed and my dad was sharing my pain adding great comfort during a wholly horrid time.

Traditionally a positive time for us this New Year was no exception. David was coming to grips with his future purpose, we were planning how to return the kids to educational stability, and I was looking after the property side of things. I had found an old, vacant bungalow with potential in our hometown that could be adapted for David.

There was one stressful problem though: I was using savings from our joint account and was only allowed by the mortgage company to buy the new house in my name because of David's condition. We always did everything together yet now David had to sign away his rights to our estate in favour of me. I felt terrible when I had to lift David's hand to lightly press the 'send' button on an email to our solicitor giving his legal consent. David normally led us as a family but now responsibility was solely mine and I had to live up to our wedding vows of "…in sickness and in health…."

The Best Place Ever

I distinctly remember on the day David was transferred to Putney the nurses asked for his clothes. I thought it harsh to expect him to wear clothes when still mostly paralysed but soon realised a simple matter of being dressed each day by the carers was critical to a mindset of recovery. Stuart had found the perfect place for David to continue his remarkable progress.

You can imagine my relief when we exchanged contracts in late January on our new house. Four hours in a car each day would soon be reduced to just forty minutes, meaning I could get more involved with David's sessions again and attend to pressing matters. I started to chase Samuel's new school place and started sourcing builders. The eventual completion day was the only day up till now that I'd not seen David yet I still felt guilty.

I started feeling confident that David would come home and not be institutionalised, but what that would look like I didn't know yet. The builders would have to be flexible towards adaptations because I was seeing David accomplish new things virtually every week.

The next couple of months had a few significant personal celebrations for us – Valentine's Day, our twenty-seventh wedding anniversary and Mother's Day. It was all very strange and not how I ever imagined celebrating each occasion with David around his hospital bed. I had lost a considerable amount of weight because of the trauma and hadn't spent any time focusing on my appearance. It was a change on Valentine's Day to make the effort with make-up and by wearing a dress, my heels clippity clopping down the corridor as I walked into the ward to see David, and I soon found my eating habits again.

He had arranged to sign his name on a valentine's card to me that his mum had bought in. We joked how childish his handwriting looked but believe me it was something so precious because I didn't know if he would ever be able to use his hands for writing again. What would those St George's consultants make of us celebrating together like this?

Could It Get Any Worse?

When Putney went into lockdown the kids and I were all in pieces. Still on my emotional rollercoaster I felt so robbed not to be able to see David and have that physical contact. FaceTime calls became our lifeline albeit we were initially dependent on the nurses keeping his phone charged and passing it to him when he wanted to call us.

New protocols were put in place upon discovery of how the virus was circulating. I found myself making visits twice-a-week to Putney to collect David's washing in sealed bags and returning them the next day to staff dressed in full PPE. It felt harsh (but necessary) to make such regular visits close to David but not being allowed to see him. We could have opted for in-house cleaning but I just wanted to be as near to him as I could. David kept me updated with the rising numbers of Covid cases, first in Putney then in his ward. Knowing how vulnerable David was, it was yet another loop on my emotional rollercoaster.

We'd got our heads together before I left David for the last time and I was going to be able to focus on the renovations and start making a phased return to work, albeit from home. Developing our outdated property was something I found great comfort in because I finally had something helpful that I was confidently in control of given our experience. This time was different though because

David wasn't around to make the quick on-site decisions that were needed or handle the paperwork. He did manage to look over Sophie's initial architectural drawings but that was the extent of his physical capabilities back then in March.

The call we hoped would never come did eventually come from his consultant at 1pm, on Wednesday the 8th of April. Covid was a deadly unknown at that stage. She told me David had taken a turn for the worse with his oxygen levels dropping, laboured breathing and not responding to nurses, so they were testing him for Covid. They were closely monitoring his position and he may be moved to St George's hospital if things deteriorated. I was experiencing that helpless 'pit of the stomach' feeling again waiting a whole day for the inevitable Covid test results.

I was thankful for being told everything that was happening but it was awful not being by his side. Waiting a few hours each time before David or the nurses could call was agony. By this time Sophie had moved back home to be with us so we could all be together as a bubble isolating through these worrying few days, not knowing how things might turn out.

When David was through the worst of Covid I had time to reflect on the past months. I discovered that stroke survivors were encouraged to learn to accept their life changing brain injuries. It is a key step in recovery and helps survivors to move on psychologically. David started to accept his disabilities early on because he believed it wouldn't be totally permanent but I was some way behind. He would often tell me assuredly about his survival from the strokes and Covid "It's called mercy when you can't help yourself."

From my perspective though I did not find it easy because it appeared that I was left picking up all the pieces. He could only focus on himself and his recovery and physically could not take on anything else outside of that. I on the other hand had no choice but to take the reins with all household and family matters. I felt I was the one left thinking how his disabilities might impact our family life, finances, and future.

Weekend Stress

When he was given weekend leave I was excited beyond words to see him again though initially I found the preparation each Friday stressful. It was a daunting role being responsible for keeping David medically safe in a building site. My capacity was pushed over the limit this time, so David and Samuel had a few chats with me to remind me to enjoy the time together and rely on other people rather than worrying obsessively about all the practicalities. They didn't want everything to go like clockwork but just for us to be together.

I was really tested on this though. I recall a Friday when the builders had knocked out the chimney breast in the bedroom that we were to be sleeping in that night. The beds were under plastic sheets to protect them from the red brick dust everywhere and the builders equipment littered the room. I pleaded with them to remove everything by 1pm as I had to leave at 3pm to collect David. Those two hours of cleaning an uninhabitable room to get it ready was a stress I never want to repeat.

I cried with relief and happiness every Friday when I picked David up because I was taking him home to our new home where he belonged. The consultants' statements about him being institutionalised were fast becoming a distant memory.

Having David around each weekend meant he could offer helpful thoughts on the renovations like old times and share in the responsibility for the decisions that were coming up. His increasing strength and capabilities meant some design decisions I would have made would have been superfluous. Initially my thoughts for design were around me being his full-time carer, which I was at first, but it was noticeable that these duties were decreasing with time: he began eating and drinking himself, getting dressed, standing up whilst shaving and brushing his teeth for example. It seemed every weekend there were improvements and I was relaxing more and more because of them.

But the greatest improvement was when he walked unaided again for the first time since the strokes. It was incredibly moving when I saw the video that had been taken of it. In the beginning none of us knew for sure if he would ever regain function of his legs let alone carry himself and take steps. The relief and excitement of where his improvements were leading was pleasantly overwhelming.

Learning to Be a Wife Again

When we were given the final discharge date for David to come home excitement and panic set in. I was beyond thrilled with having him home for good and for us to be a 'normal' family again but at the same time I didn't know what that 'normal' might look like.

In the first few days I was amazed at how well the rehab therapists had got David ready for living at home independently. He was now capable of doing even more things for himself like getting up out of bed, making himself a cold breakfast or lunch, and toileting himself. I found myself only needing to fulfil a few tasks for him each day which he couldn't do, like putting his shoe on over his cast or helping him shower standing up, because he had learned that initially struggling slowly with some things meant in time they would get easier.

I still carry the responsibilities for all the household chores, all the shopping, transport, finances, caring for the kids, paying the bills. There is a long list of jobs waiting for David when he's able and judging by his dedication to rehab it shouldn't be too many years. Only the other day his single hospital bed was taken away as he no longer needed its functionality. We replaced it with a normal king size bed of our own and were back sleeping together again. Sophie brought me in a cup of tea in bed the first morning after we started using it and when she saw us sitting up in bed talking she burst into tears crying "It's like nothing ever happened."

When I look back at the beginning of this journey, things were so bleak and confusing but now my heart has mended. I have definitely been carried closely by the Lord in so many practical ways. Now I'm learning to be less like a carer and more of a wife again.

Eighteen
In Sickness and in Health

I'm awake. That darkness is the inside of my eyelids. I don't hear The Voice. Eyelids open. My right eyelid still feels a bit heavy and everything still looks a bit funny. This is my newly decorated bedroom. Freshly painted white walls are all around me. What's through that curtainless window to my right? I'm able to turn my head this time and see clear, deep blue summer skies contrasted against rich, green palm leaves. There is no hum of activity, no whispering, just perfectly wonderful silence.

My senses are tingling with excitement and I can feel everything everywhere. I scan my new bedroom and neighbourhood carefully from my racing driver position in my hospital bed. Opposite are thin characterful detached houses 'Must be two bedroomed' I think. Only a week ago this was still our old kitchen. 'What fine surroundings' I muse. 'I'm home.'

Flattening my bed and turning to my left side I see her lying next to me for the first time in a long while. Sam's in a deep sleep and her face is as relaxed as I've seen it since this whole episode began ten months ago. Still with her youthful English rose features I haven't seen her this close to gaze at for all that time. I drink it in like a vision from another world. Fixing my gaze on her closed demure eyelids I quietly utter a word that always used to wake her "Hiya." Made with much effort against my heavy face and with as much intonation as my vocal cords will allow, my whisper has the desired effect. Nestled between her cheeks a smile appears "Hiya."

As my gaze becomes glassy I stare intently at her. "You're an incredible woman" I whisper. "Fanks" she softly jokes. With her eyes still closed she childishly says with a hint of relief "We're 'togwever.'" I feel so blessed things are working out this way – in that moment I'm okay.

Picture Postcard Church

That first week of annual leave recharged me physically and emotionally. We thought it would be good to show Sophie and Samuel their new leafy surroundings. They knew Mum and Dad's house and Big Sis's house but now they could see them in relation to other sights and sounds.

We happened to drive past the church we got married in. We pulled up outside its lich gate surrounded by willows. It's still picture postcard perfect, and the weather is as sunny as on March the 13th 1993. Sitting in silence for a while we admired its stone architecture and spire. "In sickness and in health hey bun?" I said with a raw sense of reality. Never had such short, simple vows meant so much. "Indeed – in sickness and in health" she replied resolutely.

Later in the week I got to realise a dream. The family pushed me in my wheelchair to the Thames towpath by Hampton Court Palace. I took a few steps hand in hand with Sam and stood for some staged photos taken by Sophie. It was quite an emotional moment; fortunately, I was saved from public embarrassment by my sunglasses but Sam's tears could be seen by all. When I put these photos on social media it made me realise they didn't really portray the effort it had taken to get there, perhaps giving a false reality of what was really going on. Maybe I should have put the wheelchair in the picture to convey a bit of this but I just wanted a photo of Sam and I without any 'hospital stuff' in it.

That weekend was hot, so one afternoon Sam prepared some drinks for us both, still with thickener for me of course. Putting the drinks down she stirred the thickener one last time and we drank slowly as we chatted. I finished first but when Sam came to the end of hers she had loads of globule-like gunge at the bottom. Somehow in our chatting she'd mistakenly given herself the wrong glass and I'd drunk a squash without any thickener. It was a happy accident proving I'd never need thickener again.

People Like Me

Sam directed me to join some social media stroke groups that weekend because they had given her great practical support and she thought they might similarly help me. She was right. A whole new world of encouragement, advice and tips opened up to me such that I even learnt to put a sock on with one hand from a video demonstration – very 'handy.'

There was one thing that saddened me though and emphasised again how blessed I was to have found Sam as my wife. There were a number of people in these groups who had experienced divorce or a partner leaving them after their stroke. The reasons that they were given showed a lack of understanding about strokes and seemed very selfish, ranging from "You just laze around all day" to "You're not the same person I married anymore." I felt it was tragic that people who'd had strokes and were still sick, impaired, or recovering mentally and physically weren't able to do so within the security of 'in sickness and in health.' It's the person that makes the promise.

In the coming months Julian MOURINHO, Mick and Wendy from Belvedere Baptist Church, Clive and Jane, and my cousin Richard and his wife came round to see me as Covid restrictions allowed. They hadn't seen me since before lockdown. To see me standing with a stick to greet them and sitting on a normal settee opposite them was superb. They'd seen me at most of the stages of my predicament and this by far was the most progress they'd seen.

The thing I found the most gratifying about their visits was finding out about their lives and how they were handling the pandemic. It was so nice to be involved in a conversation rather than the conversation being all about me, as was understandably the case in rehab. I'd told Giggle that this was a goal of mine because as a Baptist minister you're used to asking after others and not talking about yourself. These conversations represented a return to some sort of normality for me.

A New Normal

I'd been away from the family home and the dynamics that go with that for ten months. The family had been forced to fill the void that my sudden departure had caused with new routines and new relationships: Samuel was now the practical man of the house; Sophie was almost totally independent; Sam had total control over everything else – income, expenditure, security, design, layout, food preparation, the lot. Both Sophie and Samuel looked to Sam for advice on everything: relationships, education practicalities, careers, the list went on. Thankfully, all they expected of me was to work at my recovery. But at times I was walking around with my walker or sitting there in the room when discussions were going on and they were asking Sam for advice. Where did I fit in now?

The implications of me being around brought many feelings to the surface. Confusion was one we all struggled with. We verbalised the unthinkable - that things might be clearer if I had not survived. Yes there would be terrible grief but at least they could move on with their lives in some way. Now however, I was back home again; not really able to do anything but still having opinions and feelings about things.

The kids were struggling with a confused grief because they had lost their dad but the dad they now had was physically very different. They no longer instinctively looked to my family leadership but then I was 'coming back' gradually which added to their confusion. Nonetheless they were delighted I had survived and was home, which I could tell, but even so it was strange for us all. Chuck into all this my emotional lability and Sam's and my own confusion of learning to be husband and wife again and you've got a recipe for disaster. So we decided that family conferences were needed – not the planned type, but the 'as and when' type. If we were going to get through this adjustment time which might last a few years, we would need to make communication our top priority. I can't pretend they were easy but situations would have got way out of hand had we not had them.

There were many reminders of life before the strokes in those early months that produced tears of happiness as things started to return to a 'new normal.' Through the years Sam and I used to dart around our house laughing and joking like kids shouting, "Chase me!" We have a 'Jack and Jill' bathroom with two doors doubling up as an ensuite for us and as a family bathroom for the kids. One day I was going to the loo using my walker to get there, whilst Sam was just going out the other door into our bedroom. "Chase me!" I laughed as I walked in behind her. Immediately Sam froze and turned round, tears of gladness streaming down her face, "Those are words I wondered if I'd ever hear again" she cried.

Sleeping flat again with a duvet was another new normal. Positioned like a racing river I'd just wore a T-shirt and nappy with a towel covering my mid-riff for ten months. But with Sam asleep next to me I was more motivated than ever to get used to lying flat with a heavy duvet. It took quite a few months getting used to it by myself, but eventually Sam and I were back on the same level again. Straight away we started saving for a bed and planned for the hospital bed to go.

Relentless

I knew regaining limb strength was the key to my recovery. Now my time was free from daily sessions I was left to my own devices to form a personalised rehab programme that suited my weaker muscles. I would need to cover every part of my body except my right leg and hand. I knew one further thing – that I would not be able to keep up the intensity needed for a full day rehab programme, five days-a-week beyond Christmas. I was running on the exhilaration of being home without any carers but knew this would wear thin by the turn of the year. 'Life is a marathon not a sprint' they say and I felt I still had a few years yet to go on my fight back from paralysis, so finding a rhythm of rehab that was sustainable for that long term was key.

But initially I felt I could continue my early morning rehab routine at 6am. After a break for getting dressed and breakfast I would continue till lunch with Task Master's upper limb workouts, then afterwards do less physically challenging exercises like singing, public speaking practice, and playing Samuels drums incredibly badly. Evenings would be spent watching television whilst habitually opening and closing my left claw hand. This went on until Christmas.

My 'Beat the quads' game became full hamstring curls, lying on my front in bed, left leg standing was a firm favourite, and both my shoulders were worked too. There were many other exercises, even getting down to exercising individual fingers – I just needed strength everywhere.

None of this would have been possible without Sam who allowed my early morning bed exercises to her cost, made me my lunch and evening meal every day, and verbally encouraged me when signs of progress became evident. She did so much to facilitate and help me get better. I couldn't do this without her. It was like a parable of divine mercy. She brought such joy, hospitality, wisdom, encouragement and resourcefulness to our lives and my ministry. We were a team again. She did what she did enabling me to do what I do and in this case it was exercise.

Sometimes I would complain, thinking 'Why should I have to do this?' but those thoughts were nothing that a bit of reasoning and mind control couldn't deal with – 'If I just kept going what would I be like this time next year?' Rather than just being a goal that I had to achieve each day; exercise was becoming a way of life.

One early morning it crossed my mind to see if I could sit up from a flat position. Sit ups had taken a back seat for a while because I'd learned the technique of getting out of bed sideways. But attempting sit ups was how my gym life had all started so I was understandably curious. I managed to sit three quarters of the way up, put my right hand down behind me to struggle for the last bit, and found myself sitting up with my legs straight out in front of me. I looked around at the darkened room. 'So, this is what sitting up feels like' I thought gratifyingly. It had taken about nine months of daily sit ups to be able to properly 'sit up.' I was giddy with delight and the satisfaction uncontainable. "Sam look!" She blearily opened her eyes then smiled. "What do I do now?" I laughed. She'd watched my sit ups every Monday morning during weekend leave and understood the significance. "Don't get excited but…" she sighed through a smile as she returned to her early morning doze.

Grey Times

There were still dark times but they were becoming less frequent and not so dark – grey maybe. Most problems of disability that I faced were overcome by the inner bubbling brook I still had. But it was the practicality of life in between the strokes and 'being okay' that I was wrestling with on occasion.

Walking to the shower with my walker was cumbersome and took minutes rather than seconds and every so often it would get to me. Being driven everywhere by Sam was also difficult because my affected eyesight would be most noticeable when things were coming at me fast. Coupled with my emotional lability and dependency on pain relief tablets these things would just grind me down. Sam found me on more than one occasion sobbing quietly alone in the bedroom whilst I was getting ready for bed. "Everything's so hard" I'd sob into her shoulder.

Many nights I'd be too uncomfortable to sleep because of the muscle growth and I'd sit on the edge of my bed in darkness just staring at the radiator in front of me, 'What has happened to me?' I'd think. One morning at breakfast I even told Sam "I don't think I can live like this" when referring to how my head sensations and eyesight were making me feel 'not in the room.' The times I felt best though were when I was exercising and feeling the improvements by lifting weights, and on Friday nights after a hard week's exercise having our traditional family takeaway.

Perfect Timing

So many things just worked out perfectly for me to aid my recovery. Just one of those things was the community physio and OT support I received. They had 'accidently' left me on their waiting list when Sam had informed them I'd caught Covid in the first wave. Come early September just after I'd had my annual leave week off and planned my new routine, they called up and said my name had come up on the list to start the original rehab from April the following week.

I had OT and physio sessions for quite a few months after my return home. I showed them my spreadsheet of my daily rehab routine on their first visit. "You're just the kind of client we love," Both helpfully critiqued what I was doing, fine-tuning the effectiveness of the exercises and in some cases even making them more challenging. They helped me operate around the house and garden with tips and gadgets too many to mention, but safe to say their sessions made life so much easier.

Covid-delayed ear and eye appointments came and went. My fuzzy right ear needs a hearing aid for high frequencies and my 'not in the room' feeling is down to the brain not receiving signals properly from the upper right quartiles of my eyes. It's not easy to function confidently with this combo, especially when weird balance is thrown into the mix (for which I was prescribed special 'head' physio). It was good to get things diagnosed and good to find out things can be done to partially mitigate these effects but the doctors pulled no punches – I was going to have to adapt.

My redundant peg tube was taken out which was quite momentous. The last tube from my body was gone and I no longer felt like a hospital patient but a normal human being. All the different specialists who saw me at these appointments had to review my case and said my recovery was extremely rare. My new local stroke consultant was stunned "That is amazing. You see these scans?" pointing to his desktop showing my initial brain stem scans, "I'd expect to see you comatose for life with scans like these." I asked him why he thought I'd survived. "For one your age. Two…" he pointed upwards to the sky "…you're a Reverend, aren't you?" I nodded. "This has happened for a reason; you must tell people and give them hope." I was surprised to say the least to hear a medical professional intimate divine involvement.

Redemption

It was Monday the 2nd of November 2020 now, my 'strokerversary' as some call it. Sam and I acknowledged it but to be honest I was exercising so didn't really have time to think on it much. Besides, it was more of an encouragement for me because of my ongoing recovery than a day to be sombre. This time last year I was locked-in, paralysed, on life support, and about to have a tracheostomy, now I was using weights on my right arm, no longer needing the Therabite, had incredibly weak but full movement of my left arm, was independent around the house and bursting with purpose.

Towards the end of the month I got an email out of the blue that made me really happy. Politeness from Lewisham had got in touch. She'd set me on course for the Big Mac goal and taught me to speak again which were two huge accomplishments to her great credit. I'd often thought about her and whether she knew what a big impact she'd had on my recovery. I often thought if she could see me now she would be really satisfied in her work.

It turns out she had often wondered how I was and had seen on a computer system somewhere that I'd been discharged home after making 'some great progress.' We arranged a video chat for later that week where to her amazement she saw and heard my recovery with her own eyes - with no alphabet board in sight. Both Sam and I sat at the kitchen table recounting memories with her and expressing our thanks for her professionalism whilst telling her all about my recovery and finally eating the Big Mac.

Publishing my book 'The Majestic Meaning of Mercy' around that time was the culmination of a long journey of discovery for me. Understanding and accepting mercy had been going on since Totteridge but in recent years had stepped up a gear with the writing of this book. Just before my strokes hit it was supposed to have been self-published. So when The Voice spoke to me for the second time in intensive care and said "Leave Belvedere" I knew that the time would indeed come to be able to publish it. My new ministry of communicating His mercy was underway. The order of typing the book then having it revealed in my recovery in the most unimaginable fashion was not lost on me. As I pressed the 'Publish' button on Amazon I felt like I'd just started the rest of my life. Whenever, wherever, and to whoever I knew, I would be ministering about the depths of this majestic mercy until my dying day.

I crawled over the line to the Christmas break with my full day rehab programme for the past four months completed. It had been worth the toil. I was now able to reach my right arm almost fully up in the air and the pain had seriously reduced from my rehab days in Putney, meaning I was more adept with high kitchen cupboards. My claw hand was opening up in miniscule ways that only I would notice and similar progress was being made with my hamstring. My left shoulder was still not even strong enough to use a 0.5kg weight but I could feel the strength slowly returning. I could tell from this I would need at least a few years yet of daily rehab. My first four months at home had been slow on results but consistent in effort, reminding me of just how devastated my body had been. I'd never make it to next Christmas doing full day rehab so I decided it would be half days from the new year onwards.

By any stretch of the imagination last Christmas was odd, being locked-in yet still playing 'The bag game' with all the family laughing and joking around my bedside. This Christmas was odd too, being locked down like the rest of the country. Family gatherings were by video chat and it had not been the celebration we'd hoped for - but anything was better than last year.

I walked gingerly into the living room on Christmas morning with my walker. It was an emotional moment because the cat (promised back when I was locked-in and brought home in October) was boxing a Christmas tree bauble. Sophie didn't see the boxing match and said through tears "Are you alright Dad? It's your first Christmas home isn't it?" When the emotional lability had died down I pointed "No, look at the cat boxing!"

It was a Christmas full of 'firsts' though, and surprisingly the best was rather boring. Much to Sam's approval I started doing a few jobs around the house using my M&S basket on my walker to carry stuff. I was responsible for stocking up the toilet rolls and the shower gel dispensers we have. It might sound strange to other blokes but I was just so happy to be able to contribute to family life again by doing a few chores. Sam got her metaphorical 'to do' list out and crossed the first few lines off.

We moved optimistically into the New Year not least because my left toes had started scrunching and my left ankle was moving leftwards a bit on demand, but also because of the vaccine roll out. Categorised in the vulnerable group, we got to have them early but it would mean Sam going back to St George's hospital again. And according to the hospital map we were given the vaccine centre was right behind the dreaded café. We talked about it in advance and I felt it would be a wonderful sense of redemption for Sam to go back into that café but this time with me. We were going to see a victory out of darkness as the song had blared out last summer on her birthday weekend.

She pulled out a chair from under one of the café tables to make room for my wheelchair (it was too far from the car park for me to use my walker), and she got herself a coffee. We held hands with tears of joy streaming down both our faces as Sam uttered the sweetest prayer of thanks you'll ever hear. It wasn't the dreaded café anymore but the 'café' of redemption – it had become a special place in both our hearts now.

Now I Know How

It's been well over a year since I left rehab and Sam and I have had plenty of summer meals in pubs overlooking the River Thames. My breathing muscles are stronger now and I can talk to Sam lying down as she puts my left foot cast on every morning –

until then I'm restricted to the bed without it. My left arm can just join my right in hugging her each day with appreciation that never runs dry for her devotion.

She needn't keep an eye on me walking around the house now as my left hamstring exercises have brought a growing feeling of solidity to my stride and I'm slowly learning to ignore the diagnosed vertigo in favour of what I feel through my feet. She's still driving me everywhere, but I can transfer into the car by myself freehand while she packs my walker into the boot. Thankfully, the wheelchair is decommissioned permanently in the loft because of so much daily summer patio walking.

We spend all our days together now, not just Fridays like we used to in Belvedere, because I'm doing exercising and writing about mercy whilst she's permanently working from home. We've started attending the nearby church that I got baptised in as a fourteen-year-old. Our first time attending there was so encouraging and very different from my Putney church service experience. Standing hand-in-hand with Sam I was brimming with thankfulness and I definitely went back the next Sunday. They got wind I was a minister and asked me to preach, even though I'm still recovering. I wonder what I'll preach about.

Big Sis lives in the next village and she pops in most weeks with her own key, like my parents do as well. My dad and brothers may not kiss me on the lips now like they did when I was in hospital but I can still feel the newfound affection that remains between us. I do miss the tenderness of my parents tucking me into bed at Putney though but realistically Sam would find that a bit weird now.

They used to say all neuroplasticity was supposed to cease after a year at most but my right lower lip is now flickering on demand twenty months post-strokes. I'm glad some medics are reviewing that perceived wisdom because what would the naysayers make of my lip? That's why I still have trouble accepting I'm disabled (even though I am of course), not because I'm afraid to but because things keep changing in me. So much so I'm going to dig out Thinker's document and investigate driving again because that's looking a distinct possibility one day. It seems a world away now from being completely paralysed and Sam and I often reflect on that in amazement saying, "Was that really me?" The overwhelming wave that engulfed me has well and truly thrown me up on shore, and I'm alive to tell the tale.

I still start my morning exercise routine with the thought 'Here we go again' and still slump heavily into bed at night sighing 'I made it.' I've got my foot operation coming round in a few weeks so hopefully I can dispense with the walker totally, but my left-hand recovery needs to get its skates on, or I'll be back in the pulpit gesticulating with only my right hand.

Looking back I can see why The Voice said, "You're going to be okay" and now I also know how it was to happen; initial and immediate expert care, skilled therapists, a loving family, an athlete's mind, motivation to recover, a sense of purpose, many prayers, and of course a devoted wife, all working together for good towards His purpose of revealing His mercy.

Something outside myself did happen and my expectations were exceeded in what I believe He's done for me, making frustration a distant memory. Don't get excited but… I think I'm going to be okay.

Nineteen
Why Did It Happen?

The doctors and consultants don't know why my strokes happened but they do know what happened. I don't drink or smoke, my middle-aged spread was not enough to concern them, we have no family history of strokes, and I wasn't stressed. My heart has been checked and all the chambers and valves are fine. They have speculated on one possible cause, atrial fibrillation (which can cause clots), but there is nothing medically to prove this. I mentioned to a consultant that I thought I'd experienced what I call 'heart flutters' (irregular heartbeats) over the years but only a few times a year, but my GP in Belvedere had done an ECG for that and found nothing. My new stroke consultant at our local hospital authorised a heart monitor for a week and found nothing as well.

What happened though is not up for debate. As I understand it, I had three Ischemic strokes (a blood clot in my basilar artery, interrupting blood flow which causes cell death) in the morning affecting the left side occipital lobe (in my case affecting vision), the left side thalamus (affecting high frequency hearing in my right ear), both sides of the cerebellar area (affecting my co-ordination of muscle movements, including hands and feet, talking, muscle tone, and balance). Then in the early evening that same clot (which is why I say I had four simultaneous strokes because the same clot links them all on the same day) caused the most devastating of all strokes, the brain stem (of the pons area, which for me affected breathing, swallowing, and both sides of the body) leaving me totally paralysed and suffering locked-in syndrome.

A recent neuro and vestibular report letter sent to me from St George's sums up my case, '...he was locked-in following this (basilar artery stroke) and underwent rehabilitation... where he made a significant recovery.' This significant recovery was despite the terminated thrombectomy (surgical removal of a blood clot in an artery), which Sam was told would significantly hinder my chances of any recovery – they got that outcome wrong. Mercifully, I had the most devastating stroke in Accident and Emergency which was the best place to have it because the first four hours are crucial.

The chances of having four simultaneous strokes including a brain stem stroke and surviving like I have are too miniscule to quantify correctly. I tried to work it out recently but got lost in the zeros after the decimal point: 0.00000.... I know of just over ten people in the world who've survived locked-in syndrome (there may be more but I don't know of them) in the past ten years or so. Two of them I've spoken to online. Sadly, I also know of one teenager who has been locked-in since age sixteen and at the time of writing he's twenty-five, and I've spoken to a lady who used iGaze technology online to communicate with me who's been locked-in for twenty-five years - she was twenty when she had her stroke. I've also seen estimates for the UK of between 300-400 people at any one time remaining locked-in.

Despite the incredibly small chance of what's happened to me occurring I live each day on a plane of thankfulness that most will never know, and for their sakes I hope they never do. I want them to experience such gratitude but not to go through what I had to go through in order to experience it and I'm not sure that's possible. Every time I move my toes, or raise my arm, or swallow, I appreciate it to unspeakable levels.

Recovery journey photos are on my blog site: Revdavidhazeldine.com

Recovery journey videos are on my YouTube channel: Rev. David Hazeldine

Ministry updates on Facebook, Instagram, Twitter and TikTok: RevDavidHazeldine

Buy 'The Majestic Meaning of Mercy' on Amazon

(Left to right) Samuel, Sam, David, and Sophie together again in their new home

Perspectives

There were several key therapists and close friends who witnessed my recovery first hand. The use of nicknames throughout the book came about from a desire to respect their professional privacy. The following is their perspective on my recovery:

'Politeness,' Specialist Speech and Language Therapist, University Hospital, Lewisham

Working as David's speech and language therapist on Maple Ward at Lewisham Hospital remains the most memorable and transformative experience of my career to date. Through his unwavering motivation and dedicated support network, he accomplished recoveries which are almost unprecedented.

Much of my work was focused on the gradual weaning from his trachea during which I also supported the rehabilitation of his swallow and speech. Unfortunately for David, these interventions involved a highly uncomfortable assortment of methods, ranging from flexible cameras passed through the nostril, to reactivation of the mouth muscles using freezing cold or very sour stimuli and hours chewing on a rubbery tube to loosen his jaw.

Across his seven short weeks on Maple Ward we tried everything we could think of to support a man who initially could not move anything but his eyes and eyelids, to one who could swallow, talk, smile, and joke. It was a jaw-dropping experience (quite literally for David!) and my colleagues, and we all often found ourselves welling up, humbled by his composure and astounded by his remarkable progress day after day. Clearly this was just the beginning.

'Sprightly,' Occupational Therapist, University Hospital, Lewisham (now of another NHS trust)

One thought kept running through my head during ward rounds this particular morning with Mr Hazeldine: 'How do we encourage daily occupations or goals with a patient who can only move his eyes?' I clearly remember meeting Mr Hazeldine for the first time. During my initial assessment he had no movement in his head, neck, legs, or arms. He could only blink his eyes for yes/no answers. I had to clearly ask only simple, closed questions. One of the things that surprised me was that he was cognitively aware about his situation.

Mr Hazeldine had an extremely supportive family who were always by his side from the first day on the ward. One of the first questions that Mrs Hazeldine asked was how they could be involved in his rehabilitation. I educated Mrs Hazeldine on how to complete passive range of movement exercises for Mr Hazeldene's' arms, which she started completing daily. One day Mrs Hazeldine reported to therapists that she could feel some movement in Mr Hazeldine's' hands. On my assessment it was amazing to feel some flickers in his muscles and gradually he could squeeze his fingers and participate in bending his arm.

'Cobbler,' Physiotherapist, The Royal Hospital for Neuro-disability, Putney (now of another NHS trust)

David's recovery has been remarkable, and I feel truly honoured to have been a part of it. To go from initially being considered 'locked-in', to walking out of hospital really is a testament to his sheer determination and ability to find ways to complete his own therapy outside of therapy sessions - the famous Reverse Plank! As the book recounts, David's journey through rehab was not all sunshine and rainbows but to have been able to assist getting him home to his wonderful family really brightened up the dark days of working in healthcare during a pandemic.

'Task Master,' Occupational Therapist, The Royal Hospital for Neuro-disability, Putney (now of another NHS trust)

David always asked questions about our interventions but participated in everything that we asked of him once he knew why. Things don't always go according to plan in rehab, but David was always so positive and resilient. It was so lovely getting to know him and Sam and I think that the support from his family and friends really helped him. It was brilliant that he was able to spend time at home with his family at weekends during the latter part of his stay at the RHN, which could not have been achieved without the determination from him and his family. His personality and previous life experience definitely helped him in his rehab journey.

'Giggle,' Speech and Language Therapist, The Royal Hospital for Neuro-disability, Putney

Never have I met a man so motivated, so driven, and so focused on his rehabilitation goals. Even when David was in pain, feeling tired or feeling low he participated and gave therapy his all. This book pays homage to the relationship between patient and therapist, one that both parties must nurture, respect, and find joy in.

'Tunes,' Music Therapist, The Royal Hospital for Neuro-disability, Putney

David presented aware and alert with dysarthria, characterised by right-sided lip weakness, velopharyngeal insufficiency, and reduced breath support. David consistently engaged with our sixteen sessions, responded positively to all my suggestions even with exercises outside of sessions. His breathing patterns improved to a normal diaphragmatic dominance along with reaching his breath control, vocal intensity, and pitch range goals.

Stuart Hazeldine (older brother and on behalf of the family)

David's strokes were the most traumatic event our family has been through. Unpredictable and rare with a highly uncertain outcome, we were thrown upon our faith and each other to sustain us through his many months in multiple hospitals recovering from one of the most extreme physical disabilities a person can suffer. Our shared belief that the providence of God could bring David more healing than the doctors ever expected, combined with David's deep determination to make the most of every gain as it arose has brought us to where he is today – a quite miraculous recovery from the brink of death.

Mick Harvey, friend and Elder, Belvedere Baptist Church

God took David from being a vibrant, outgoing, much-loved husband, father, pastor, and friend, to a locked-in, ventilator dependent victim of the most severe stroke which normally would have ended his days. From the hospital's prognosis of "we expect another stroke soon from which he will not recover, but even if he did he will remain locked-in and on a ventilator" David is progressing towards almost full physical recovery and is a living demonstration of the mercy of God. There has been no bitterness or recrimination against God; instead, David has allowed the strokes to deepen his understanding of His ways.

Clive Urquhart, friend and Senior Pastor, Kingdom Faith Church

Walking into the intensive care unit it felt like being surrounded with impossible circumstances. Seeing David lying there and locked-in two things came to mind; 'God does the impossible' and 'Be healed in the name of Jesus.' We anointed David with oil and spoke a blessing over him, that God's face shining towards him brings order out of chaos and breathes new life into him to enable him to arise and fulfil his God given purpose. Since then we have watched the unfolding story of God's mercy as David's body has responded to treatment alongside God's healing nature and power at work.

Julian Sanders, friend and Elder, Hope Church, Orpington

To watch David's miraculous recovery from someone who could only talk to me via the blink of an eye and an alphabet board to being able to walk 5km in a day (with a walker, so far) raising funds for The RHN is an amazing joy to me. It is an absolute privilege to count David as a friend but more importantly a true brother in Christ.